the dailymash
Annual 2013
MIND CONTROL PING-PONG

Edited by Neil Rafferty

Written by:
Tim Telling, Nick Pettigrew, Tom Whiteley, Neil Rafferty, Steve Morrison, Matt Hawkins, Jennifer McKenzie, Suzy Houston, David Stubbs, Mike Bollen, John Camm and Will Maclean

Mash Books

Launched in April 2007, the Daily Mash is Britain's biggest humour website providing a daily diet of spoof stories, commentary and opinion on national and international news and sport.

www.thedailymash.co.uk

Mash Books

First published in the UK in 2012 by Mash Books, an imprint of Mashed Productions Ltd and The Daily Mash.
www.thedailymash.co.uk

ISBN 978-0-9566662-5-3

A copy of the British Library Cataloguing in Publication Data is available from the British Library.

Design and picture research:
mICHaEL GiLL DesigN LtD.
www.michaelgill.eu

Except pages 6, 30, 31, 50, 62, 76, 85, 96 and 110:
Courtesy of False Advertising
www.fadvertising.co.uk

A book that needs batteries

Popular, despite being pointless. p7

Jubilee Special Reports

Nation celebrates 60 years of Rolf Harris

pages 12, 48, 49, 51

New Festival

100% twat friendly
page 3

the dailymash

ww.thedailymash.co.uk   **PROUD SPONSORS OF THE LEVESON INQUIRY**   Monday 2012

Yay woo yay the Queen wooo yay

What's really striking here is Her Majesty's kind eyes

WOO, the Queen yay woo, according to lots of people

THE people are very happy. The Queen has been better than them for 60 years, because she has a massive house and a special hat.

When asked what he liked about the Queen, crowd member Tom Logan said: "Yay woo yay, the Queen, yay.

"Woo?"

Meanwhile, as preparations are made for things involving soldiers and flags, geriatric men who rarely see daylight have been repeating phrases.

Old man on television standing next to a river Sir Stephen Malley said: "Sense of duty, changing times, sixty years, national treasure, carriage."

Another old man on television, Sir Roy Hobbs, said: "Who could ever be cynical in this time of woo yay."

Mother-of-two Emma Bradford was less enthusiastic. She said: "It's hard to say exactly how good she is because there's no other Queens of England currently working that we can compare her to.

"I mean, I might have made an even better queen. It's something I mentioned to the careers advisor at school but he just made a face and gave me a leaflet about jobs in data entry.

"Still, I don't want to be difficult so…woo yay, the Queen.

"Yay."

Why would you think pension strikes are about pensions? asks TUC

TRADE Unions are to press ahead with pension strikes because the strikes are not about pensions and never have been, it was confirmed last night.

Despite key concessions which would allow millions of public sector workers to continue doing nothing when they retire, the TUC said the strikes must go ahead because the government is full of people who live in Downton Abbey.

Brendan Barber, Lord of the Unions, said: "These people are different from me. They talk like BBC4 and went to a school with a rowing team.

"Some of them own a horse. They are not of my tribe."

Barber said the pensions issue went back to May 2010 when the party he had been bribing lost a general election to the party being bribed by the Lord of the Banks.

He added: "At that point strikes were inevitable and the government's latest offer completely fails to acknowledge the extent to which I constantly imagine them guffawing at racist jokes about women.

"Plus, I'm all geared up for a strike. I've written a speech full of brilliant jokes about Ian Duncan Smith that I want to deliver though scratchy megaphone from the back of a flat bed truck.

"All the girls will think I'm really cool."

Nathan Muir, an industrial relations analyst, said: "When the right is in power the left goes on strike. When the left is in power the right keeps turning up for work.

"It's almost as if some of them are still just a bunch of fucking students."

Angry emails 'a threat to traditional bollockings'

> The accomplished bollocker can channel the primal rage of the riverbank

BOSSES' increasing reliance on irate emails or 'e-bollockings' is leaving them incapable of delivering face-to-face put-downs, it has been claimed.

Research by the Institute for Studies has found that 84% of UK bollockings are simply moody emails.

In most cases the sender will betray no outward signs of anger, appearing absolutely fine five minutes after sending when he or she walks past the recipient's desk and asks if they're coming to the pub later.

Professor Henry Brubaker said: "Traditionally, underperforming employees would be summoned into the boss's office – sometimes even seized by the arm and physically dragged – where they would be shouted at for up to three hours with repeated use of the phrase 'fucking useless' and possibly even a mug being hurled.

"The e-bollocking, although sometimes effective especially if delivered in BLOCK CAPITALS, is a relatively meek affair. Given the choice, I think most people would rather work for a prick than a spineless prick."

Britain has a distinguished history of bollockings. The biggest ever recorded bollocking was that given to 13-year-old baker's apprentice Tom Logan in 1666, for a cake-burning fuck-up that resulted in the almost total destruction of London.

Professor Brubaker said: "On a recent research trip to China I saw bollockings far more accomplished than anything we in the UK are currently capable of.

"There's this factory owner called Mr Pang,

he literally just walks around the shop floor shouting, regardless of whether anything's even fucked up. I suppose you'd call it pre-emptive bollocking."

Some company executives who are worried about their diminished shouting-at skills are enrolling on booster courses.

Kitchen tile company boss Stephen Malley is halfway through a 13-week Bollockings and Borderline Bullying Refresher Course, run at his local college by retired football managers.

He said: "Today we've been learning a technique called 'firing a few fucks into them'.

"It's much more gratifying than simply sending an e-mail."

New festival is aimed directly at twats

If Alex James is not there it's because he's trapped under one of his own pigs

THE Magic Fox Vintage Smoothie Boutique Urban Forest Pop-Up Chill Retreat is to be Britain's first 100 per cent twat-friendly festival.

As the festival-marketing season begins, the organisers of the new event claim to have concocted the ultimate pretentious weekend for utterly dreadful people.

Festival 'curator' Tom Logan said: "My friends and I wanted to create something for ourselves – a right bunch of wealthy jumped-up media twats with a ridiculous sense of entitlement and legions of horrible mop-headed children, all of whom are called Mungo.

"We would probably get punched at Latitude. Honestly, we're that bad.

"Magic Fox Vintage Smoothie Boutique Urban Forest Pop-Up Chill Retreat is a combination of all the most annoying, smug, po-faced aspects of festival culture into a smorgasbord of heavily-branded twatness.

"There will be deerstalker hats, depressingly nostalgic 90s dance acts – we'll probably go with Faithless, who are now old enough to be considered ironic – and some fucking thing called The Mystic Dell.

"We've got people with moustaches playing gypsy jazz records on a gramophone while the Wombles perform a burlesque routine, stupid fucking food stalls where you can buy a 'hand-raised' pie with an infantile name, and luxury woodland play areas where horrible designer-clad infants can kick frogs while giggling.

"It will be a hybrid of Waitrose and *The Wicker Man*.

"Also there will be macaroon biscuits. And people wearing fox masks, just prancing around aimlessly."

He added: "But the Magic Fox Vintage Smoothie Boutique Urban Forest Pop-Up Chill Retreat isn't just about twats. There's also plenty for pricks, like a bicycle-power retro puppet eco-show that reworks Punch and Judy as an environmental fable.

"There will be stalls. We don't know what they'll be selling but everything will be a tenner."

Music fan Emma Bradford said: "I'm going to spend that weekend in West London as it will have become temporarily pleasant."

Elderly parents reveal plan to buy shit computer

YOUR ageing parents are planning to get themselves a 'computer with the internet' this Christmas, in a move that will ruin your life.

It is likely that they will use a shopping catalogue to purchase a machine that is described as 'easy-to-operate, great for first-timers' and represents very poor value for money.

The news came during a telephone call where your mother explained that although they had never wanted a computer before, looking at websites might be quite interesting especially as the telly is so poor lately.

Also your father may be able to get the dog's special shampoo cheaper online than from the vet, who sells it at an extortionately high price.

Your mother said: "I went to a shop with your father and the man said they've all got the internet on them now. Is that right?

"He showed us one but I didn't like the keys, they were all I don't know."

She added: "You can help us set it up. You know all about that sort of thing. It'll be fun."

The government has recently come under renewed pressure to ban the sale of computer equipment to the over-60s.

Technology writer Tom Logan said: "It's all very well to encourage 'silver surfers' with nauseatingly upbeat television adverts.

"But just try explaining to a 68-year-old lady that people don't actually post photos to Google in an envelope then tell me it's still a good idea that she 'got connected'."

'ALL MARVEL CHARACTERS ARE GAY' REVEALS DC COMICS

IRON MAN, the Hulk and all other Marvel comic characters ever have been outed as gay by rival publisher DC.

Comics giant DC teased fans earlier this week with the revelation that a popular character or characters would be revealed as homosexual.

However fans had assumed the publisher would out some of its own characters, rather than those of its highly profitable competitor.

A DC spokesman said: "Our industry has to reflect changing times and diverse lifestyles, even if the bulk of its readership is heterosexual young males.

"I can exclusively reveal that pretty much all the characters in the Marvel universe are gay.

It is, in fact, a gay universe.

"We applaud how Marvel has taken the very brave, progressive approach of being pretty much 100% homo-tastic, in the full knowledge that its audience may shrink considerably.

"The Avengers secretly run a leather bar called Crooze where the Hulk works as a gogo dancer and Spiderman serves drinks topless. Also Captain America wears a thong under his costume.

"Thor meanwhile likes burly, hairy lumberjack-type men with very thick necks. And enjoys being naked with them and kissing them all over their bodies.

"Really Marvel comics are the ideal comics to read if you are

gay, or if you want all your school friends to think you're gay. And we at DC are so proud of their bravery.

"We only wish we'd thought of this inspiringly progressive approach first, but unfortunately nearly all our DC characters are resolutely heterosexual."

However a Marvel spokesman said: "While we remain committed to representing social diversity in our comics, DC would not be saying this shit if *Avengers Assemble* hadn't just smashed it at the box office.

"Mostly our characters are not gay. They're asexual. And we hope they continue giving inspiration to the asexual community."

Hulk angry,
Hulk never
meet nice guys
only bastards

Leaving child in pub 'right for Britain' says Cameron

DAVID Cameron has insisted that leaving his nine year-old daughter in a pub is the sort of tough decision that will rescue Britain from recession.

The prime minister left Nancy in a pub near Chequers after the move was agreed during a conference call with chancellor George Osborne and Nick Clegg, the self-styled 'deputy prime minister'.

Mr Cameron then used an iPhone app about fancy handbags to distract his wife Samantha while special branch body guards hustled everyone except Nancy into a big car and sped off.

A Downing Street source said: "When Samantha realised Nancy was missing she went straight into David's study and told him to go and get her.

"She was standing over his desk shouting 'Right. Fucking. Now'.

"But he just shook his head and said that while it was a painful decision he could only go and get her when market confidence had been restored."

The source added: "Samantha kept saying 'what if something happens to her?' but David said that George Osborne had looked into it and assured him there was no reason to believe that anything bad would happen to a child left alone in a pub."

A Treasury spokesman added: "Britain is a safe haven."

It's not a right if you're stupid

Number of people going to university almost back to where it should be

THE number of young people going to university could soon be the same as the number of young people who should be going to university, it has been confirmed

Latest figures from UCAS show a steep year-on-year decline as more school leavers realise that just because universities exist it does not mean they automatically have to go to one of them.

A spokesman said: "It seems the prospect of £9,000 a year in fees has made many people realise that university is actually quite an important thing to do.

"So if you are going to spend that kind of money you should probably mean it."

Roy Hobbs, professor of university studies at Roehampton University, said: "Over the last 20 years public policy has been focused on finding new ways for young people to do nothing.

"It now seems that one of the ways of doing nothing is being priced out of the market. It may sound like science fiction, but perhaps in 20 years time young people will get proper jobs after doing something."

Wayne Hayes, 19, from Stevenage, said: "It occurred to me that universities should be about academic excellence rather than giving me somewhere to stand around quoting the Mighty Boosh for three years.

"I am not remotely interested in any of the things that are taught at university and so I've decided to offer my services free to a local business for 18 months where I can get some experience, learn how to do an actual thing and not spend twenty-seven grand so some bonged-up nonce with a doctorate can teach me how to watch television."

The UCAS spokesman added: "As long as this trend continues we may also see the number of universities drop to below a million."

'God particle' does not believe in God

THE particle named after God last night stressed it was not religious in any way.

Higgs Boson, a 14 billion year-old particle from the absolute centre of the universe, used its first fleeting contact with humanity to reject the notion of an omnipotent space wizard.

Mr Boson said: "I only have a trillionth of a second to say this so I want to be crystal clear – I am not a God-botherer.

"I'm not saying for a fact that God does not exist, but as everything you can see, smell, hear, touch or experience in any conceivable way is, to all intents and purposes, based on me, I can tell you that 'God' was not responsible for what I like to think of as my essential 'mojo'.

"If God exists then, given that I'm pretty much everywhere all the time, there's a fairly reasonable chance I would have bumped into him by now. But so far, it's just me and the particles to which I give 'mass'.

"And I know that 'mass' is ironic given all those Popes who existed because of me and who then burned people at the stake for suggesting that I am not the work of Satan.

"Me and some other particles you have not even begun to imagine laugh about 'mass' all the time. It's funnier than a cat falling off the back of a sofa in a hilarious universe that without me would have been a never-ending void that's not even dark because there'd be no such thing as darkness."

Mr Boson added: "The only relationship I have with Satan is via any of the atoms that humans use to express the idea of Satan.

"That's not to say I don't go to church. If you're the thing that makes everything in the universe exist then you can't really avoid it.

"But rest assured, I sit at the back, read a Richard Dawkins book and giggle about how clever he thinks he is."

"Michelangelo got it wrong"

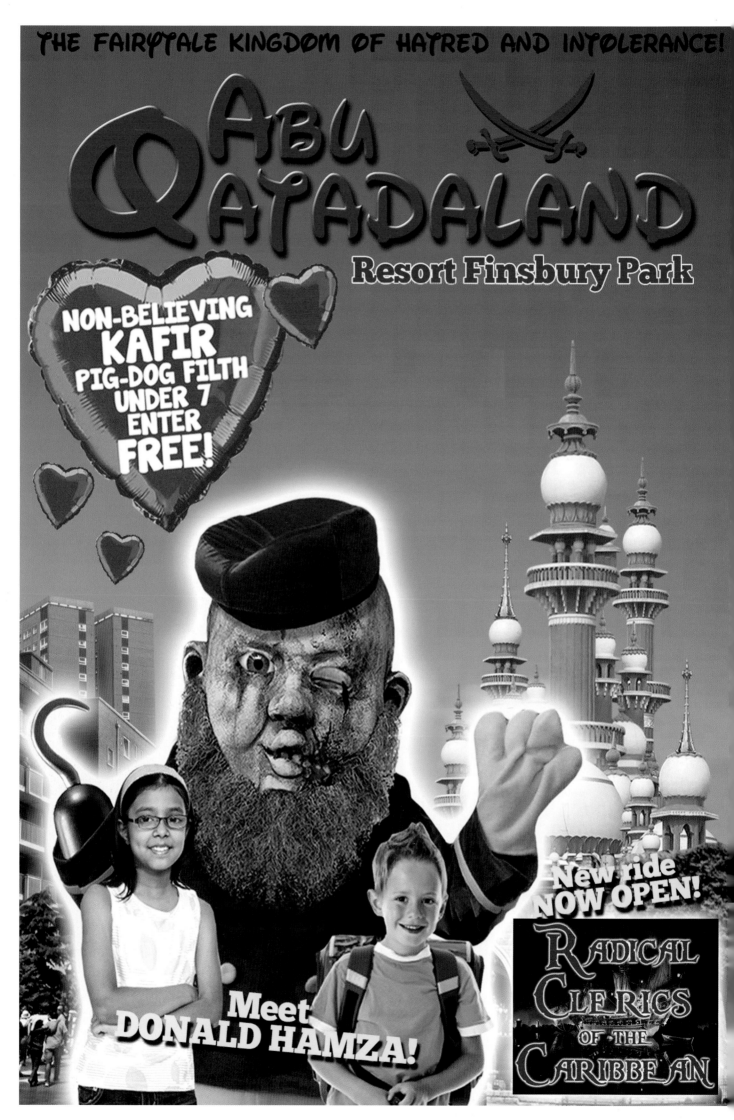

Battery-powered book a surprise hit

A type of book with a battery has proved popular despite being pointless.

The Kindle electronic book does essentially the same job as a book, except it looks shit and you sometimes have to plug it in.

Despite this, the device has proved a huge success, mainly with menopausal women determined to maximise the amount of Lynne Truss they can consume in a day.

Technologist Nikki Hollis said: "Have you ever been reading a paperback book and thought, this is a nightmare, the design of it is awful, just doesn't work at all?

"Exactly.

"Despite this someone took it upon themselves to create a book with a screen and buttons, effectively mimicking the tedium of computer-based toil, but in your leisure time.

"Apparently it's really convenient for going on holiday because you don't have to carry lots of books. But unless you're Brian Sewell, how many books are you really going to read on holiday? One and a half, max.

"Although with the electro-book you can strap it into a black leather carrying case so it looks like an S & M Gameboy, which is quite funny.

"Otherwise it's like a proper book that got shot up by criminals and rebuilt as a soulless machine called robobook that is always sad and has lucid dreams about the halcyon days when it was made of paper.

"Still, it's really caught on. Probably because of how much humans like to buy new things."

Electro-book fan Emma Bradford said: "Thanks to this gadget I've been able to get rid of all those books that were cluttering up my house and making it look interesting.

"I'm really excited about the drab, unemotional future age we are entering."

Millions remember martyrdom of Saint Pancake

CHRISTIANS worldwide have remembered the martyrdom of St Pancake of Antioch, who was stuffed full of hot cheese, fried and repeatedly thrown into the air around 530 AD.

Pancake grew up in rural Turkey, and quickly acquired a reputation for good works.

But it is the manner of his martyrdom at the hands of the church for which he is best remembered, and today his death agonies will be re-enacted by devout millions worldwide.

Religious commentator Stephen Malley said: "We know very little about St. Pancake's life, but a great deal about the brutal manner in which he was dispatched.

"He was beaten and battered, then stuffed with a large quantity of cheese.

"Although some historians differ on this point, and insist it was spinach and ham.

"Either way St Pancake was subsequently fried, on both sides.

"After which he was repeatedly tossed into the air, in a cruel mockery of his belief that he might one day ascend to heaven or, as Pancake described it in his text De Recipus, "the righteously-made shalt adhere to the celestial ceiling."

As a final indignity, Pancake's body was smothered in lemon juice.

Warhammer more than just a hobby, says Miliband

He could defend this country from a troll attack

FANTASY battle game Warhammer is a serious military simulation, according to Labour leader Ed Miliband

Recent revelations about David Cameron's 'chillaxing' weekends have sparked debate about whether politicians should have enough spare time for leisure pursuits.

But although Ed Miliband is a regular Saturday fixture at his local Games Workshop, when he can be seen painting tiny metal balrogs with a group of small boys, he claims Warhammer is not a hobby.

He said: "It's quite the opposite of 'chillaxing' – rather it is a military simulation of the type practiced by great leaders since Roman times.

"I don't even enjoy it, I do it from a sense of responsibility.

"For example last week I confronted the moral complexities associated with weapons of mass destruction when I used a siege catapult on some elves.

"The fantasy context does not appeal to me especially. The game could represent any theatre of war – Afghanistan, Iraq, Iran – it just happens to be populated by highly detailed miniature orcs with hand-painted banners.

"Obviously though if my mighty chaotic orc battalion causes a puny elf army to rout and flee there's a certain frisson, I won't deny it."

He added: "I also sometimes attend steam fairs in a work context, because it's important to connect with voters who might otherwise be mistaken for paedophiles."

Graduates forced to take jobs that match their skills

'UNIVERSITY' graduates are increasingly having to take unskilled jobs commensurate with their lack of ability.

Figures from the Office for National Statistics show that the average wage for someone with a British university degree has fallen to pretty much where it should be.

Professor Henry Brubaker, of the Institute For Studies, said: "The fact that 20% of new graduates are unemployed says less about the current job market and more about the age-old problem of fucknuts.

"Nevertheless our higher education system continues to do its job of producing people who can round-up shopping trollies without supervision."

The study showed that the best paid graduates were those with degrees in medicine, dentistry and other things that actually need to be done.

Meanwhile, trade unions have demanded a halt to graduates taking unskilled jobs, insisting they do not want to represent people who are even worse than public sector workers.

Holly Turnbull, a 2:1 from Roehampton University, said: "I had some nebulous plan that my degree in Heaven 17 would translate into a six-figure income but all I have to show for it is a heartbreakingly predictable tattoo.

"I was explaining this the other day to an old friend I sneered at for leaving school at 16 to become a plumber. But he just jumped into his Audi while asking if I would like to clean his bogs.

"He has seven of them."

Women told to plan ahead for ill-judged drunken sex

WOMEN are being advised to prepare for the aftermath of having sex with someone they hate.

Health advisors are recommending that women draw up a Christmas check list including alibis, emergency contraceptives and 'crying time'.

Dr Emma Bradford said: "Start by checking your diary, and noting all the events where free alcohol will be available. We call these 'regret points'.

"Be honest and ask yourself 'am I going to fuck up and do something that makes me hate myself?'.

"If the answer is 'yes', 'past form indicates a strong possibility' or 'I might do if there is low lighting and they play that Bryan Ferry song I like', then you need to get everything in place for the fuck-up.

"It's vital to ensure that the following day you have set aside at least an hour for crying.

"Plus another two hours for calling your best friend from work and asking them to fill in the details of the previous night including how many people noticed that you were definitely going to have sex with the person you had sex with.

"This advice also applies to men just replace the word 'crying' with 'exaggerating'."

THE Mashipedia EMERGENCY FACT SERVICE

With WIKIPEDIA once again laid low by chronic indignation, the Daily Mash has unselfishly stepped into the breach with a list of Top Ten Must-Have facts:

1 Benedict Cumberbatch was born Cumberdick Bendybatch. He changed it because he thought it sounded weird.

2 The Costa Concordia is a huge metaphor for Italy because it formed an alliance with Hitler during the second world war and has won four World Cups.

3 Humans are not designed to understand the phrase 'complex carbohydrates'.

4 Richard Dawkins became an atheist after Gloria Hunniford befouled his Segway.

5 The Eurozone crisis has already been solved but Brussels Eurocrats don't want you to know.

6 In today's ultra-competitive jobs market, the best way to secure long term, lucrative employment is to tell the interviewer how much you enjoy uploading quirky cat photographs to icanhascheezburger and using the word 'cunt' on Facebook during office hours.

7 Goldman Sachs owns your house and at some point they are going to want it back.

8 'Anal sex' was the 73rd most popular search term on Wikipedia last year. It was mostly Republican candidate Rick Santorum getting himself into an angry froth.

9 Sherlock Holmes faked his death by hiring a BBC film crew and two of the people who write *Doctor Who*.

10 This article is our intellectual property, if you steal it we will RUIN you.

Your problems solved, with *Holly Harper*

Dear Holly,
I referred to my boss as a flatulent twatlord when talking to one of my colleagues the other day and unfortunately she was standing right behind me. She seems to have taken it on the chin, but I've been nervous about going home because my boss also happens to be my wife. Shall I just pack a bag?
Simon, Rutland

'Boss-eyed spunk-badger'

Dear Simon

I think bosses and teachers must be quite similar because my teacher, Mrs Dodkins, wasn't delighted when someone wrote 'Shirley Dodkins is a boss-eyed spunk badger' on the whiteboard in huge red letters. She was even more distressed by the revelation that the jibe was written in indelible marker, meaning that, six weeks later, the phrase has inadvertently become a kind of class motto, daily emblazoning the space above Mrs Dodkins' head as she recites the five times table. But some kind soul has also jazzed up the corner of the slogan with a tiny bum doing a poo, so all in all it really is a thought-provoking piece.

Hope that helps! Holly X

Your astrological week ahead, with Psychic Bob

Aries
21 MAR-19 APR
The ability to empathise with the suffering of your fellow man and perform acts of truly selfless altruism is what separates us from our primate ancestors. Fancy a banana?

Cancer
21 JUN-22 JUL
It's very easy to sit at home criticising the likes of Peter Kay and Michael McIntyre, calling their comedy clichéd and lazy and bemoaning a general public that bovinely eats the whole unappetising mess up. So crack on.

Libra
23 SEP-23 OCT
Treat yourself to one piece of chocolate a day during your diet for all your hard work. Of course an entire bar counts as one piece, you absolute superhero.

Capricorn
22 DEC-19 JAN
While leaving your body to the local medical school is a laudable gesture, in your case it's actually rather unfair. Even to students.

Taurus
20 APRIL - 20 MAY
People accuse you of being obsessed with sex and that's true, but only in the same sense drowning people are 'obsessed' with oxygen.

Leo
23 JUL-22 AUG
It's not unusual for a doctor to ask for a stool sample but it is generally considered bad form if they do it on a first date.

Scorpio
24 OCT-21 NOV
After the success of post-work restaurants 'Thank God It's Fridays' you launch a chain of depressing drinking holes called 'Fuck You Satan, It's Monday'.

Aquarius
20 JAN-19 FEB
Things turn out better than expected this week as your four-day stand-off with the police ends not in a hail of bullets but in the light drizzle of a good kicking.

Gemini
21 MAY-20 JUN
This week, in a strange case of life imitating art, everyone you meet will be balding with curly hair and singing *Bridge Over Troubled Water*.

Virgo
23 AUG-22 SEP
When your eyes meet across a crowded bar, a nod, a wink and a wiggle of the eyebrows is all you need to do to let her know you've got chronic Tourettes.

Sagittarius
22 NOV-21 DEC
What with judgement day coming up and the four horsemen of the apocalypse roaming the land, now may not be the best time to start making gay porn to pay for your crack habit.

Pisces
20 FEB-20 MAR
A long, hearty laugh can be as beneficial to your health as a workout in the gym so why not save membership money by shoving a pensioner into the road twice a week?

GARY BARLOW TRAPPED IN QUEEN'S ARSE

SURGEONS are working to free Take That toady Gary Barlow after he became wedged inside the Queen.

The singer and organiser of Buckingham Palace's Diamond Jubilee Concert had been fawning over the monarch during a meeting about what colour trousers Madness should wear. When she fell asleep, he clambered into her backside.

Unfortunately his passage into the Queen's body was blocked by antipodean lickspittle Rolf Harris, who already resides in her colon where he has a permanent studio. Surgeons now have less than 24 hours to remove Barlow from Her Majesty's lower intestine before jubilee celebrations begin.

Doctor Stephen Malley said: "Barlow has somehow become wedged sideways in the Queen, I think because he was trying to punch and kick Rolf Harris.

"We're trying to get a rope around his torso so we can drag him out like a calf."

He added: "Ordinarily we would let Gary Barlow pass through the Queen's body naturally or with the aid of mild laxatives, but given the impending celebrations we have to be more aggressive.

"This weekend the world's media will be focused on the Queen, and were she to give rectal birth to a middle-aged man in the midst of it all there would be an absolute furore.

"Also of course Barlow would then technically be a prince, and the Queen would have to give him a county and a special soldier outfit, neither of which he deserves."

The unfolding events

1. The Queen's arse.

2. Mr Barlow inside the Queen's arse.

3. Mr Barlow discovers long term blockage, antipodean entertainer and artist Mr Harris

4. A fight ensues over ownership of said colon.

5. Surgeons will today attempt to rectify the situation.

'Onesies' prove men no longer in existence

THE availability of one-piece romper suits for adult males proves that men are over, it has been claimed.

Experts believe that the man-sized baby grow or 'onesie' is the concluding event in the history of human masculinity.

Evolutionary biologist Dr Emma Bradford said: 'The modern world's diminished need for physical strength has left men struggling to adjust. Or even, it seems, to put on a pair of proper trousers.

"Penises may exist for another couple of generations, but thanks to the onesie the concept of 'man' is officially dead."

She added: "Technological advances mean that is in now pretty much possible to make a baby from silicone.

"Given the choice between a petri dish full of translucent matter and a genital organ that has been in a fluffy orange jumpsuit, I'm going with the fertile goo and my antique vibrator."

Human male activities prior to dressing as giant infants include eking a living from the soil with bare, bleeding hands, forging tools from white-hot metal and fighting vagabonds to the death with swords.

Historian Nikki Hollis said: "As recently as 1946 it was not uncommon for men to do brave, dangerous things.

"Today, human males are bouncing around music festivals clutching falafels and shouting 'Tigger's here, weeeeeee!'.

"It's over."

Tom Logan, a 28 year-old onesie wearer, said: "Me dirty bot-bot. No nice. Wipey bot-bot. All stinky poo.

"Bot-bot!"

Jesus Fucking Christ Almighty

Frozen Planet 'gave whisky to penguins'

EMPEROR penguins in the hit wildlife series *Frozen Planet* are given shots of whisky so they act-up for the cameras, it has been claimed.

An insider at BBC Bristol said their suspicions were first aroused when, alongside the usual specialist camera equipment, the group's baggage also included 60 bottles of Tesco own-brand Scotch.

The whistleblower said: "The thing that you have to remember about most wildlife is that it's piss-boring. Penguins especially.

"They normally just stand there and make a weird noise most of the time. We have to give them a bit of encouragement otherwise all the Baftas would go to ITV.

"So all that endless 'fighting over territory' they do is just bollocks. What usually happens is after nine hours of fuck all, the cameraman gives them two fingers of whisky.

"You'll be surprised how quickly they start 'fighting over territory' at that point.

"And that thing they do when they 'regurgitate food for their young' is not really regurgitation. It's actually caused by the fact that penguins are not supposed to drink whisky."

The source added: "I've got a friend at the Discovery Channel who says the dancing ones are all fucked up on Mephedrone."

Emperor penguins: pissed

Can we get Flash now? ask Apple owners

OWNERS of iThings have asked if they can get Adobe Flash Player now.

Amid emotional tributes to Apple genius Steve Jobs, millions of customers said it would probably be okay for the company to go ahead and install the video playing software because Jobs would never know.

Technology analyst Julian Cook said: "We have lost a great man. An innovator and a visionary who changed the world and stopped me watching videos on this thing I paid more than four hundred quid for.

"That said, I have had my iPad for nearly a year now and every time I use it I still think, 'fuck me, this thing is amazing'.

"I doubt there is another person in history who has provoked as many 'fuck me' moments as Steve Jobs. From the iMac to the iPod and iPhone, to *Toy Story, Wall-E* and *Up*, it's just one 'fuck me, how are they doing this?' after another."

Cook added: "His legacy will mean the company continues to grow and innovate, though I suspect many people will now find it easier to complain to Apple because Steve Jobs always looked like he might shout at you."

Meanwhile many Apple devotees are relaxed about Jobs' death, insisting he will rise again, probably on Sunday afternoon.

Tom Logan, who never doubted or denied Jobs, said: "He will then be taken up, at which point we, as disciples, would ordinarily go forth and take over the world. However Steve had already taken care of all that. Somewhat comprehensively.

"He actually makes Jesus look a bit 'meh.'"

Jobs was first to realise that the original iPad was far too big

Italian cruise captain rode moped and pinched arses on sinking ship

THE captain of the Costa Concordia abandoned his post to buzz around the deck on a Vespa sexually harassing female passengers, it has emerged.

As the Italian courts ruled that the disaster was now an official metaphor for their country, it emerged that Captain Francesco Schettino failed to follow emergency procedures and instead sat around drinking expresso chain-smoking and inviting panicking women in life-vests to come over and sit on his dick.

Magistrates are also examining claims that when the ship was headed toward the rocks the captain leaned on the ship's horn, stuck his head out of the side window and screamed at the island of Giglio to get out of the way.

The allegations are not the first to be made against the captain, who in 2009 was reprimanded for idling his ship outside a coastal convent, where he revved its six diesel engines at sexy young novices and suggested they put their fat titties in his mouth.

Costa Concordia passenger, Francesca Johnson, said: "I saw the captain most days on board and he'd always thrust his hips at me, say 'This ship? Is mine.'"

Eyewitness accounts suggest the captain at first threatened the rocks the ship struck with vengeance from his 'Uncle Cesare and his friends who you don't want to fuck with, eh' but when he realised the ship was sinking changed sides and claimed he had supported the rocks all along.

Wanker: a once innocent term now ripe for reclaiming

Stylish
Masturbator

with
Dermot Jaye

THE seminal blob on Rachel Weisz's Balenciaga frock is so small as to be practically invisible.

It's a miniscule grey wisp, Casper the Friendly Ghost as viewed on Google Earth. But the security brute – at an LA launch event for an exciting new maple-conditioned cognac – is immune to reason and determined to punish me for my wayward DNA.

I consider explaining how manhandling me will affect his life chances and how I am actually a personal acquaintance of La Weisz following a relaxed and intimate nine-minute interview for a major lifestyle quarterly (she bakes and isn't afraid to get rough in the boudoir). But it's late and I'm tired and it's all way too cliché. "You dirty fucking wanker," bellows the door brute, handily throwing me down some steps towards a waiting taxi.

Back in my accommodation – an exciting new boutique hotel teeming with hip hop aristocracy – I watch a documentary about sharks, sip a free cognac miniature and ruminate on the negative connotations of the word 'wanker'. Like 'negroid' or 'batty man', it is a once-innocent term now ripe for reclaiming.

The modern world has forgotten that masturbation can be an aspirational activity. A man with a lot of literal and metaphorical spunk needs to deposit it regularly, whether into a woman, an imported marble sink, or onto the sequinned hem of a Hollywood power-MILF.

Many of history's greatest males were

also its biggest wankers. Churchill was known to close associates as 'Winst-onan' because of his voracious masturbatory appetites.

Frank Sinatra was an avowed self-pleasurer who once bespoke a box of 400 monogrammed silk 'single-use bedside handkerchiefs' from his Savile Row tailor, and was known to calm pre-concert nerves with bouts of solo love lasting up to seven hours.

And it is a open secret in Downing Street that the 'dried wax' on Dave's office floor is the result of 'burning his candle at one end'.

Work hard. Play hard. Wank hard. This is my credo. I consider my bouts of self-stimulation not as lonely and pathetic, but

a vigorous, defiant act of firing my seed into the universe. Mating with the elements, if you will. The ultimate expression of masculinity – look out world, here I come!

I am a writer, an editor, a paragon of the modern male, a polymath and a polyglot. But perhaps most of all, I am a wanker.

Dermot Jaye is founding editor and masturbator-at-large of Stylish Masturbator magazine.

Online comment-writers to get their own internet

A NEW internet is to be created for people who like writing comments, so everyone else can enjoy surfing the web without their torrents of bile.

The new web, dubbed 'Masturnet' after users' penchant for literal and metaphorical self-indulgence, will be just pictures of things with the question 'Why do you hate this?' underneath.

Google-built algorithms will reward commenters by adding random numbers of Facebook Likes or retweets, giving users the false impression that they're not just screaming their repugnant semi-literate vitriol into an ocean of white noise.

Paid moderators will occasionally pretend to be the celebrities or writers that are being commented on, appearing 'below the line' while acting chastened and educated by the commenters' wise words.

Meanwhile normal people will be able to enjoy sending worthwhile messages and watching iPlayer dinosaur documentaries on a much faster version of the good internet.

Tom Booker of the Better Internet Federation said: "The internet is the greatest advance in human culture of the last 30 years, so why must it be dominated by geeks purple with fury about a

This man's extensive masturbation experience makes him a font of knowledge

review that lowered the overall score of *Avengers Assemble* on Metacritic?

"We considered various options, including simply sawing off the bottom half of the internet and dumping it at sea, but this seemed the most humane."

Following the announcement, regular Mail Online commenter Vajazzle81 wrote: **"GIPSYS get mi TAXES for FREE HOUSES & EUSSR traitors shud HANG & Kim Kardashian is a FAT BITCH."**

Corporate bitch I now am

£10 for signed photo it is

ONCE-GREAT Jedi Master Yoda will flog anything for cash, it has emerged.

Yoda, full name Richard Yoda, has issued a statement offering himself for television or radio adverts, after-dinner speaking and 'corporate levitation gigs'.

He said: "My services available to anyone they are, if right is price. Basically pimping my wrinkled green ass I am.

"If you want lightsabre stunts, extra that will be. My agent you will speak to, deal agree we shall.

"Seen the light I have. Either live in crappy swamp can I, teaching Jedi knights 2.7 credits an hour max or make easy money advertisements, live in loft apartment.

"Also then more fanny will I get than I can shake my gnarled stick at. No-brainer, it is."

Many fans see Yoda's sell-out as the final insult to the memory of a franchise now consisting largely of insults to its memory.

Jedi obsessive Roy Hobbs said: "Yoda's involvement in the grubby world of product endorsement is the final nail in the coffin of my 55-year-old ongoing childhood. I haven't been this upset since the holiday special."

However an unrepentant Yoda said: "Do or do not do. There is no try.

"Unless you try the delicious taste of Sugar-Frosted Wheets, the light breakfast cereal that kids love!

"Twenty grand I get for saying that. Very nice too that is."

Bankrupt nation makes wonderfully thoughtful gesture

GREEKS SAY SORRY WITH HUGE HORSE

The beautiful horse was left outside the European Central Bank in Frankfurt

LEFT outside the European Central Bank in the dead of night, the horse has now been moved into the ECB's central lobby where it is proudly on display.

A gift tag attached to the horse, which is surprisingly light for its size and has small holes along the length of its body, suggested that it should be placed in the bank's vaults overnight to avoid it being targeted by thieves.

Mario Draghi, President of the ECB, said: "How nice of the Greeks to acknowledge the trouble we've been put to on their behalf with this wonderful horse, handmade and so large it could hold a dozen double-decker buses.

"The card with it, which had a teddy bear dressed as a hobo on the front, explained that Greece made us this because they don't have enough money for a present, which brought a tear to my eye.

"Nonetheless, unless they can somehow find €200 billion overnight then austerity measures must continue."

Oddly, Greek representatives in Brussels have hinted that they may soon be in a position to settle their debts and have puzzled the French and German banks that hold their loans by asking if there is any discount for cash.

The government of Spain has reacted angrily to the gift, accusing the Greeks of trying to bribe the ECB and redoubling their own efforts to weave a gigantic sombrero-wearing straw donkey.

Everyone lying about how great their weekend was

EVERYONE in Britain will today lie like a bastard about making the most of the sunny weather.

As the country baked in record breaking temperatures no-one will admit to finishing Sunday as a badly dehydrated, drunken catastrophe.

Martin Bishop, from Stevenage, said: "I'm going to say that I had a few friends over for some Provencal rosé and barbecued langoustines, but actually I opened a bottle of own-brand vodka, stripped naked and fell asleep on my neighbour's garage roof.

"My penis looks like a mini saveloy. I wish I was an Eskimo."

Stephen Malley, from Finsbury Park, said: "I'm going to say I took part in a really nice, chilled-out afternoon session in the beer garden of the Duke of Cumberland when in actual fact it was a thick, wet, heaving mess of bright-red borderline alcoholics who are not built to withstand temperatures above 14 degrees centigrade.

"I'll claim that my girlfriend and I wandered home in the warm evening air and made love with the window open when in reality I think I may have glassed an old friend of my sister's after she dripped sweat into my grappa.

"And yes, I may well have pissed myself, but I'd been wearing the same underpants for 72 hours so who the hell knows?"

Helen Archer, from Hatfield, said: "I am going to say that my attractive friends and I drove to the Norfolk coast in our Fiat 500s and then played rounders, drank cava and ate some ratatouille before singing Boo Radleys' songs around a campfire.

"I actually made myself a big pot of melted cheese and watched six Harry Potter films on the trot with the curtain's shut.

"I got this healthy, sun-kissed glow from thrusting my head into a basin full of hot Dettol."

This did not happen anywhere

Ukulele market crashes

THE second-hand value of a ukulele has plummeted to £1.12 after thousands simultaneously lost interest in the stringed instrument.

Experts had predicted the crash – which follows a year-long 'speculative uke bubble' during which legions of middle-aged men took up the inexpensive instrument in the hope it might make them feel alive again – although they have been shocked by its severity.

Tom Logan, musical instrument market analyst at Donnelly-McPartlin, said: "All the conditions were right for a perfect ukulele storm.

"First, the number of ukulele players in the UK now far exceeds the demand for ukulele recitals, which despite being exaggerated by enthusiasts and Frank Skinner, is almost non-existent.

"The glut of uke players has devalued ukulele proficiency so players are no longer considered cool, if indeed they ever were.

"Add to this the uke owners who have simply lost interest organically, after having achieved sufficient mediocrity to strum *When I'm Cleaning Windows* quite slowly.

"This triggers a mass offloading of ukuleles onto eBay, into car boot sales and in some instances even free ads papers.

"We had hoped that Britain' current obsession with all thing vintage and 'retro' may have bee enough to sustain the ukulele. Bu sadly not.

"And I don't think the market ha bottomed out yet. Expect to se former ukulelists in the street, try ing to swap their instruments fo potatoes."

The current uke crash is th first major instrument catastro phe since Recorder Wednesda in 1993, when millions of schoo children simultaneously quit th simple wind instrument after tir ing of the one-note tune *Bus Bee*.

Six months ago, a decent quality beginner-level ukulele with case was valued at £45.

Britain's Biggest Bollockings Volume 1

> "I've **told** you a fucking **million** times you fucking stupid **fucking FUCKER.**"

For the first time ever on DVD, 40 of the UK's best-ever tellings-off, presented by Richard Hammond.

Rare footage of Britain's underperforming workers 'getting a few fucks fired into them'.

Bollockings include:

- 'Mrs H sent a really important invoice to the wrong address'
- 'Mr Y blocked his boss's car in then left work early to go to the pub'
- 'Ms P is 15 minutes late for a presentation, for the fifth time in a row, because she got drunk the night before'
- 'Mr R pulled the alarm cord on the disabled toilet thinking it was the flush – he shouldn't have been in there in the first place and now they've got to get someone to come from fucking Bristol to reset it'

90 expletive-packed minutes of shouting, belittlement and tears

PLUS:
An exclusive 15-minute reconstruction of the lost classic: 'Mrs Thatcher tears strips off Alan Clark because of numerous balls-ups'

£19.99 in all good stores

the dailymash

www.thedailymash.co.uk

TELL YOUR CHILDREN TO SHUT UP

May 2012

OUTRAGE OVER REACTION TO CLARKSON REACTION REACTIONS

Your opinion about his opinions is the most important thing in the world

BRITAIN was trapped in a 'death spiral' of infinite complaints last night.

The e vortex of indignation began just after 7pm when Jeremy Clarkson, the country's highest ranking oaf, presented, without a hint of irony, his detailed plan to shoot public sector workers in front of their families.

Within moments Tony Parsons, the official Left-Wing Clarkson, said people who criticise public sector workers were Nazis while John Prescott, the former Lord High Oaf, said his successor was guilty of a 'hate crime'.

In turn Parsons was accused of outrageous anti-Semitism while Prescott was forced to deny being deputy leader of the Khmer Rouge during the 1970s.

Seconds later the country

was straining at the limits of its 140 character allowance in a bid to react to the reaction reactions in a way that was guaranteed to provoke a reaction.

Bill McKay said: "People who compare strike critics to Nazis should be gassed and cremated as part of a huge, secret plan to wipe out Nazi-comparers."

Helen Archer said: "Any-one who thinks Nazi-com-parers should be gassed is worse than Jeffrey Dahmer and should be raped in prison three times a day."

Nikki Hollis said: "People who say Nazi-comparers are worse than Jeffrey Dahmer want to rip my mother's heart out, eat it and puke it into a bucket which they...[new tweet] ...will then use to paint the front of my house."

Meanwhile Tom Logan who suggested that Clark-son's original comment was perhaps, an advert for a DVD, was accused of being a member of the Ku Klux Klan.

Logan also suggested that instead of reacting to Clark-son reaction reactions we should, perhaps, come up with some stuff we can sell to foreigners before we all end up busking in front of each other.

His house was then burned to the ground.

Last night a spokesman for the United Nations said: "Britain needs to go fuck itself in the face."

BBC apologises for making Piers Morgan look comparatively good

THE BBC issued an official apology last night after comments by Jeremy Clarkson made it possible for Piers Morgan to appear relatively human.

Clarkson's now-infamous One Show comments about striking public sector workers created a two-hour window in which Piers Morgan was able to leap on Twitter and register his outrage, and thus temporarily look better than someone else.

A BBC spokesman said:

"We apologise unreservedly for inadvertently creating a digital portal through which Piers Morgan was able to clamber back into the human race, aided by his oddly endearing use of the word 'twerp'.

"Measures are currently being taken to ensure that Piers Morgan's temporary veneer of decency loses its sheen as quickly as possible. By Piers Morgan."

Piers Morgan said: "The second I saw Alex Jones bite her lower lip, you'd better

believe I was straight on Twitter, like a virtual rat up a virtual drainpipe.

"Or more precisely a reptile, going up whatever reptiles go up.

"You have to remember that opportunities like this don't come along too often. I mean, what else other than Clarkson is less beloved than me?

"The sound of fingernails down a blackboard, huge crab-like spiders and Chlamydia, perhaps, none of which is likely to ever make outrageous comments on a family television show."

Football cameramen threaten strike over 'SEXY WOMAN'

TECHNICAL staff covering Euro 2012 have asked for more pay to continue filming attractive female spectators.

The specialist 'girl finder' cameramen responsible for picking out the young, pretty women in cropped replica tops from amongst the hordes of potbellied racists believe their skills should be rewarded with a 25% bonus.

Girl finder cameraman Roy Hobbs said: "I've been doing this job since the 80s, when you were lucky to find a single woman in the stadium that wasn't built like James Corden and dishing out meat pies, so I've earned it.

"If our demands aren't met, people at home hoping for a bit of cleavage will have to make do with Adrian Chiles' shirt gaping open when he leans forward."

NUTS, the National Union of Totty Spotters, which represents professions including 'girl finder' cameramen and dating website home page editors, believes that the skill of locating a single pair of jiggling breasts in a crowd of 10,000 stocky males is undervalued.

A spokesman said: "Our members train for years by covering the golf. Once they can track a white ball against a grey sky from half a mile away,

Bingo

they are ready for the challenge of finding a human-looking England supporter."

The union are pressing for a sliding scale of bonus depending on the event and the nationality of participants involved, with a darts match in Essex earning the full tariff to a Brazilian beach volleyball

match actually requiring wages to be deducted.

Hobbs said: "If we've had no agreement by 5pm today, coverage of the England match will still go ahead but expect to see many sudden close-ups of Wayne Rooney's sweaty, balding pate that may make you retch into your Doritos."

BOAT RACE KILLS 27

THE 158th Varsity Boat Race between Oxford and Cambridge ended in a shootout which killed nine participants and 18 spectators.

After a tedious start involving a protester in a wetsuit, the Cambridge cox drew a 9mm handgun and opened fire.

The gunshots provoked immediate retaliatory fire from the Oxford boat, killing three rival rowers before the Cambridge crew brought their vessel's 50mm cannon into play, holing Oxford amidships and wiping

Oxford's Dr Alexander Wood was shot in the neck with a crossbow

out sections of the elite crowd.

The Oxford cox, holding a concussion grenade in each hand, leapt from the bow of his boat toward Cambridge but was cut down by rifle fire in mid-air. However it became clear this was only a diversionary tactic when the Cambridge boat was reduced to matchwood by

mortar fire from the bank.

The mortar then misfired, killing its crew and spectators, including a galaxy of famous Cambridge alumni, and leaving the crews to fight hand-to-hand in the muddy water of the Thames.

Four died of knife wounds and drowning before an Oxford rower,

clutching the splintered remains of an oar, crossed the finishing line and his university were declared the winners.

Sir Steve Redgrave, commentating on the race for the BBC, said: "What a wonderful showcase for British sport in this Olympic year.

"The pageantry, the tradition, and the savagery of those young men is an example to us all. I rescued a severed arm from the riverbank and will be mounting it in my home."

Hugh Laurie, a Cambridge rowing 'Blue' and the elite star of *Stuart Little 2*, said he was honoured to be asked to formally execute the surviving members of the losing team on the famous 'quad' of Trinity College.

John Terry dedicates Champions League win to himself

Terry now plans to spend a few days gazing at his reflection in a pond

JOHN Terry's single-handed capture of the Champions League trophy was especially for John Terry, it has emerged.

Speaking from his eighteen-bedroom mansion built in the shape of his own face, the pathologically-confident Chelsea defender also suggested his England team mates need not fly out to Poland as he has this one covered.

Terry said: "When John Terry beat Barcelona, many said John Terry couldn't repeat that effort against Bayern, but they underestimated how much it means to John

Terry to make John Terry's dreams come true.

"John Terry can now take this form into the Euro 2012 tournament and face some of the best non-John Terry teams in Europe to win John Terry a trophy for the first time since 1966.

"They think it's John Terry? It is now."

Meanwhile, Chelsea caretaker manager Roberto Di Matteo has been told he will need to cure a major disease to secure the job permanently.

After winning two trophies and making Chelsea play like they've actually met each

other before, Di Matteo felt confident of being offered the role but it's understood Roman Abramovich is looking for something a bit more Nobel-Prize-winning-y from the ovoid-faced Italian.

Di Matteo said: "I was given the alternative task of making everybody in the world not want to punch John Terry in the face with a fist made out of threshing machines, but boxing off cancer seemed a more realistic target.

"I think I am ideal for the role but I know I face stiff competition from, well, you can probably guess who, can't you?"

IT'S NOT THAT MUCH FUN, SAY HORSES

HORSE racing is okay if you are in the mood, horses said last night.

As the nation's favourite horse-killing race claimed two, horses across the country urged humans not to assume that they know when a different species is enjoying itself.

Tom Logan, a 14 year-old horse from Stevenage, said: "Most of us quite like a bit of a run now and again, but not all of us and not as much as you think.

"For instance, my half-brother Geoff is a fat, lazy prick.

"Of course that doesn't stop some lower middle class bitch clambering

on top of him twice a week and thrashing his arse with a stick.

"I said to him 'Geoff, Max Mosley pays good money for that'. He told me to go fuck myself."

Logan added: "I'm fond of a gallop, but on my own terms, d'you know what I mean? And, put it is this way, if I wake up and find myself in the mood for a jog do you think I really want to have a little Irishman sitting on top of me while I do it?

"Do you think that makes it perfect?

"Anyway, just make the fences smaller, you fucking dicks."

"You don't know anything about me" said Logan

Housing benefit withdrawn from anyone with under £25 million

THE Conservative party has unveiled new plans to cut housing benefit and income support for anyone with less than £25 million in capital holdings.

The new threshold, which ministers are calling the Decency Benchmark, will ensure that poor people with regional accents won't be able to get their filthy hands on taxpayers' cash, which will instead be channelled to wealth creators to spend supporting the economy.

Prime Minister David Cameron said: "Giving the wealthy even more money sends a clear message to society that poverty doesn't pay and will encourage those people being persistently poor to stop it at once."

The changes will make housing benefit only available to those with three or more homes but will increase the average amount paid from £90 per week to £9,000. Income support recipients must provide evidence of their company directorships.

Cameron added: "How would you feel if you were BAE Systems and you were told Sorry, we can only afford to buy 8 Warrior armoured fighting vehicles this year because we're paying a bunch of 18-year-olds to live apart from their abusive alcoholic parents?'"

Under the new proposals, the less wealthy would be forced to live with their parents until they have proper jobs, which could create a generation of men who have weirdly obsessive relations with their mums, like in Italy.

24-year-old Stephen Malley said: "I've already gotten to the point where my mother's opinion about my girlfriends is more important than my own.

"Also I am boasting to all my friends about her pasta sauce, despite it only being Spicy Tomato Ragu, and have become quite fascinated by transsexuals."

Zuckerberg with his head of design

Myspace spots gap in market for old version of Facebook

FORGOTTEN social network Myspace is to stage a comeback by using the version of Facebook that everyone thought was absolutely fine.

Executives spotted a gap in the market after Facebook redesigned itself in a way that makes it virtually unusable.

A spokesman said: "The old Facebook design was so good. It made us look like amateurs. But, as Facebook doesn't seem to want it anymore, we figured there was no point in letting something that did not need to be changed in any way go to waste.

"We're just so happy that Facebook has suddenly decided to stop being good at this. Seriously, we'd cleared our desks."

Industry analysts said the market was surprised at Facebook's decision to turn itself into a complete and utter mess shortly before its initial public offering, but stressed that it is irrelevant because the company's value is based on a weird dream where Mark Zuckerberg kills 100 billion chickens.

Martin Bishop, head of bubbles at Donnelly-McPartlin, said: "Dot-com valuations have been based on weird dreams since the mid '90s. If it ain't broke don't fix it."

The Myspace spokesman added: "It'll be like Myspace and Facebook have done a Freaky Friday body-swap. Hey, let's all share our memories of the original version of Freaky Friday using the Freaky Friday Myspace App.

"You see, we are still incredibly bad at this, but at least the Freaky Friday Myspace App Status Update will not keep moving from one side of the page to the other for absolutely no reason."

BENEFITS CLAIMANT ADMITS SUBSISTENCE INCOME SCAM

AN unemployed man is scamming the taxpayer out of £67.50 a week, it has emerged.

Former care worker Norman Steele does not have to lift a finger to receive the sum, equivalent to an annual salary of £3,510, which he uses to pay for a lifestyle of utility bills and Lidl sausages.

He spends his time sitting at home filling out job applications, or lounging in front of his 14-inch full-colour TV.

Steele said: "The best part is watching the *Secret Millionaire*, where the participants get to stay for a week in a flat that is supposed to illustrate grinding poverty but is still bigger and nicer than my place."

The UK's sizeable embittered population were eager to criticise Steele's perceived 'like something from Shameless' benefits bonanza.

Sales manager Wayne Hayes said: "For some reason I can't seem to grasp the fact that £67.50 a week is a very small sum of money to live on. This fucker probably drives a top-of-the-range BMW and eats unicorn steaks every day."

Factory worker Carolyn Ryan said: "The thought of other people having any amount of pleasure, however minimal, makes me sick. My life is utter shit so I don't see why everyone else's shouldn't be too."

Ms Ryan then used the phrase 'end of', as though that in some way validated her argument.

Her friend Emma Bradford said: "Some people on the dole are lazy bastards that do fuck all. I know this because I'm one of them.

"But that doesn't stop me having a worthless, vindictive, judgmental opinion, and it is as follows: they should complete at least 900 job applications per day while wearing lead clogs."

He enjoys a rich tomato sauce on his pasta shapes

France is basically Hitler, agrees everyone

FRANCE has once again proved itself to be exactly the same as Adolf Hitler, everyone agreed last night.

The nation of malodorous collaborators was condemned after just under one in five of them expressed views held by at least one in five people in England.

Marine Le Pen, leader of the extreme right wing National Front, took 18 percent of the vote in the presidential election, causing Britain to reach for its large, foam pointing finger.

Using the big finger to type its editorial, the Daily Telegraph said: "France is once again teeming with

Let us now return to pointing it at Greece

Hitlers. According to our calculations that now means that everyone in Europe is a Nazi. Bad thing. Immigration. Churchill."

The Guardian then used the finger to add: "Le Pen's resounding vic-

tory is a dark day for social democrats like Francois Hollande. We can only hope that when she is sworn in as Fuhrer later today she does not have him executed."

But as Le Pen pushed French sup-

port for fascism to it highest leve since 1941, experts stressed that he manifesto may as well have had a Essex accent.

Julian Cook, professor of Britis logic at Roehampton University said: "While the French tend to pu their paranoid racists in one pot w like to spread ours around. Som BNP, a splash of UKIP and a dollo of ghastly working class Labour.

"But, overall, we prefer to keep th vast majority of them in the Conser vative Party."

Margaret Gerving, a retired head mistress from Guildford, added "The French are a bunch of stinking lazy xenophobes. I'd sooner trust a idiot Mick."

DJs Fabio and Grooverider announce residency in rave retirement home

PENSIONED-OFF Radio 1 drum and bass dons Fabio and Grooverider are to become resident DJs at a home for retired junglists.

The seminal breakbeat icons, real names Fabio and Grooverider, lost their weekly slot at BBC Radio 1 when the station shuffled its DJ roster to reflect the tastes of five or six years ago.

However they have since announced a residency at Milton Keynes' new junglist retirement home, Rave Meadows.

A spokesman for the DJs said: 'Rave Meadows is a specialist care home for ageing ravers who want to continue partying but in a secure environment with nurses on hand to feed them, change their toilet pads and take care of any mental health issues.

"Fabs and Groove will be on the decks from 10am-3pm every day in the recreation room – also known as 'Arena One' – with a one-hour break for lunch and 'rave refreshments'.

"They will be rinsing all the classics from the golden years of pirate radio so expect copious rewinds."

He added: "Residents are permitted to blow their horns and whistles, within reason. But if it starts to do our heads in they may be confiscated."

Rave Meadows resident Tom Logan said: "I've been raving for 20 years and I'm 84 now, or at least that's how old I look.

"So this is the perfect arrangement for me – hot drinks and sponge baths on tap, regular drugs and a constant onslaught of heavy duty drum and bass."

Nurse Emma Bradford said: 'Sometimes the residents can be challenging as they are mostly quite doddery and insane.

"But it's so rewarding when the DJ drops a big tune like the VIP dubplate mix of Champion Sound and they all hold their lighters in the air."

Britain to be hit by entirely typical weather

During winter snow can often reach the ground

TEMPERATURES in the UK are going to fall sharply over the coming weeks because that is what happens at this time of year, it has been claimed.

Meteorologists believe that winter, a spell of short, cold days commonly defined as a season, will be more or less exactly what you would expect.

Professor Henry Brubaker of the Institute for Studies said: "Household fuel costs will rise considerably as families try to increase the temperature of their homes.

"People on the verge of death may die.

"Ice and snow will create icy, snowy conditions.

"Your car will refuse to start.

"Because it's winter.

"It's really nothing to freak out about, unless you're a pre-Neanderthal cave dweller who believes sunsets are caused by Gark, the angry moon god."

He added: "There's a high probability that this winter will be followed by another sudden, weather-related phenomenon known as spring."

Housewife Nikki Hollis said: "The important thing is to stay inside, carry a flaming torch at all times and don't be sentimental about eating your plumpest child."

"Their hooves touched. 'You've always been the filly for me,' snorted Richard through his nosebag as he tenderly brushed a bluebottle off her hind quarters with his tail."

Horse Romance

Horse Romance is the world's leading publisher of equine love stories. If you like the idea of horses in turbulent, exciting love affairs, you'll love Horse Romance.

Titles include:

Stablemates
The New Stallion
A Paddock Too Far
Dark Filly
A Tail in the Wind

Why I am leaving the Empire

by Darth Vader

Today is my last day at the Empire.

After almost 12 years, first as a summer intern, then in the Death Star and now in London, I believe I have worked here long enough to understand the trajectory of its culture, its people and its massive, genocidal space machines. And I can honestly say that the environment now is as toxic and destructive as I have ever seen it.

To put the problem in the simplest terms, throttling people with your mind continues to be sidelined in the way the firm operates and thinks about making people dead.

The Empire is one of the galaxy's largest and most important oppressive regimes and it is too integral to galactic murder to continue to act this way. The firm has veered so far from the place I joined right out of Yoda College that I can no longer in good conscience point menacingly and say that I identify with what it stands for.

For more than a decade I recruited and mentored candidates, some of whom were my secret children, through our gruelling interview process. In 2006 I managed the summer intern programme in detecting strange disturbances in the Force for the 80 younglings who made the cut.

I knew it was time to leave when I realised I could no longer speak to these students inside their heads and tell them what a great place this was to work.

How did we get here? The Empire changed the way it thought about leadership. Leadership used to be about ideas, setting an example and killing your former mentor with a light sabre. Today, if you make enough money you will be promoted into a position of influence, even if you have a disturbing lack of faith.

What are three quick ways to become a leader? a) Execute on the firm's 'axes', which is Empire-speak for persuading your clients to invest in 'prime-quality' residential building plots on Alderaan that don't exist and have not existed since we blew it up. b) 'Hunt Elephants'. In English: get your clients – some of whom are sophisticated, and some of whom aren't – to tempt their friends to Cloud City and then betray them. c) Hand over rebel smugglers to an incredibly fat gangster.

When I was a first-year analyst I didn't know where the bathroom was, or how to tie my shoelaces telepathically. I was taught to be concerned with learning the ropes, finding out what a protocol droid was and putting my helmet on properly so people could not see my badly damaged head. My proudest moments in life – the pod race, being lured over to the Dark Side and winning a bronze medal for mind control ping-pong at the Midi-Chlorian Games – known as the Jedi Olympics – have all come through hard work, with no shortcuts.

The Empire today has become too much about shortcuts and not enough about remote strangulation. It just doesn't feel right to me anymore.

I hope this can be a wake-up call. Make killing people in terrifying and unstoppable ways the focal point of your business again. Without it you will not exist. Weed out the morally bankrupt people, no matter how much non-existent Alderaan real estate they sell. And get the culture right again, so people want to make millions of voices cry out in terror before being suddenly silenced.

'In a flash of inspiration, I emptied a bowl of Wotsits into my hair'

One Woman's Week

with Karen Fenessey

This week, I was guest speaker at the local Brownies annual fundraiser.

I decided to focus on the drivel young girls are raised to believe these days. Romantic vampires, virgins, one armed TV presenters – what happened to tales of yore about simple, shoeless maidens whose beauty never went unnoticed by the wealthy king who duly plucked them from obscurity and lived happily ever after in his massive sparkly palace? All my expectations of life and love were dictated by the Paul Daniels Magic Show and I was literally suicidal when it stopped in 1994.

I was immediately disconcerted to look out upon a sea of airbrushed wrinkle-free faces and impossible curveless bodies – most of whom I couldn't help notice were going braless. There were no fat ones and only one or two dark skins thrown in. I was disgusted at the message this was sending out about the two most maligned minority groups in society. Girls need to know that their edgy looks and controversial facial styles shouldn't dictate what kind of organisation they swear into. They are being brought up with impossible dreams of perfection and I am humbled to admit I am part of the problem.

I had to show them the Karen they're so desperately trying to emulate is not the definition of perfection they all imagine. In a flash of inspiration, I emptied a nearby bowl of Wotsits into my hair and announced, "See? Even Beyonce doesn't fall out of bed looking perfect."

My audience of gawping, slack-jawed brutes hadn't understood. Thinking on my feet, I whipped my pants down to give a rare showing of what my fifth form biology teacher giddily referred to as my Mambo Number Five. "Do you think this just magics itself into an exclamation mark every three days? No – it takes hard work and dedication." I did a little plié to let those at the back see. The gasp that went around the room proved I'd finally got my point across and everyone was in awe of my true humility and womanhood.

At this point, Brown Owl stood up and tried to cut me off. I let out a cry, realising what it's like to be Adele every single day. If this Owl demagogue thought she could use her knotting skills and position with Jesus to usurp me, she had another thing coming. As she set about thanking me for my time, I pointed at her and began loudly hissing. I'd never tried this technique before but had seen cats do it in my garden and it always seemed to work for them. And sure enough, after 15 minutes she sat back down.

I was a little hoarse by this point but was still able to wrap up with a heart rending performance of *Someone Like You,* which I dedicated to the memory of Paul Daniels.

New Bond film to involve large amounts of paperwork

THE new Bond film will feature unprecedented levels of admin, according to its makers.

Skyfall will follow James Bond as he looks to broaden his CV with experience in line management and budget-setting for the Met Office.

Director Sam Mendes, who denied the new bureaucracy-heavy direction was influenced by a reduced production budget, said: "The story opens with M stopping Bond from publishing figures for the annual mean rainfall for Carlisle.

"He goes rogue and releases the data at a meteorology convention in Penge, with departmentally explosive results.

"I don't want to reveal too much of the plot but I'll just say two words – 'disciplinary' and 'hearing'."

Star Daniel Craig has completed a punishing six-month regime of measuring average precipitation – then collating the data into a detailed report – in preparation for the highly bureaucratic thriller.

Other possible indications of cost savings are the replacement of the iconic Aston Martin with a 2002 Ford Focus pool car for which the former spy has a petrol card, and the announcement of Michaela Strachan as the film's key love interest.

Q will still provide gadgets to help Bond complete his mission, but fans may be disappointed to learn that one of them is a back support for his swivel chair.

Daniel Craig said "I'm going to be spending the next four months pretending to look at Powerpoint presentations and frowning a lot.

"It's far more authentic and gritty than any of that camp old Bond nonsense like shagging supermodels in zero gravity, I think audiences will appreciate that."

Bond's pen is also secretly a pencil

Madonna becomes new face of Tena Lady

Do this with confidence

AFTER a near perfect performance at the Super Bowl on Sunday, Madonna has been unveiled as the new brand ambassador for feminine leakage pads.

Millions of viewers around the globe watched in awe as the 72 year-old Queen of Pop defied the laws of gravity and decency as she power-danced like a crazed nursing home hooker in spandex.

Dressed in black thigh high boots and a tiny dress, the veteran of vogue thrilled her audience with frequent glimpses of her flawless, hardened gusset which she waved from side to side like a sinister and menacing totem of war.

Gynaecologist, Dr Linda Graham, said: "At her age, you'd expect Madonna to be leaking fluid like an annoying, drippy tap.

"But she magically appears to have the pudenda of a 22 year-old, with not a prolapse or wizened vulva in sight. I am sure there are millions of pensioners out there who want to know her secret."

A spokesman for Tena Lady said "Our product is undergoing a revival, thanks to an ageing population and the magical qualities of herbal tea.

"Now inspirational women like Madonna are breaking down social taboos and making it more acceptable to encounter elderly genitalia in the public domain."

LOADS OF PEOPLE LIKE TOTALLY AGREE WIVAT PISSED BIRD ON THE TRAM

Niricoogara is bordered by Hordundas and Crostaricrua

THAT pissed bird on that video, right, was like totally spot on, wun't she, it was confirmed last night.

EVERYONE'S sayin' like, you know, maybe she shouldn't have been swearin' so much wiv a little kiddie on her lap an' all that, but she wun't far wrong wuz she.

This bloke Dave, who does a bit of plasterin' for Big Andy, said: "I fuckin' can't get no fuckin' job cuz of all them Nicoogaragruans. Fuckin' everywhere int they?

"I wanna work. I fuckin' do. I wanna work.

But there's always some fuckin' Nicaroogaran who gets the fuckin' job instead of me just 'cause they turn up on fuckin' time and can say 'Nicragugarra.'"

Steve, who's been doin' that Mandy from the pub, added: "That bird on the tram, right, where wuz all the English? Where wuz all them white people that should have been standin' up for her? Ain't no fuckin' English

left now is there?

"Maybe I'll go to fuckin' Niroogacargua and take their fuckin' jobs."

Meanwhile, get this right, the fuckin' rozzers have only gone and nicked her cuz she wuz speakin' what we wuz all thinkin' wun't she.

Dave's mum said: "I just feel sorry for that little kiddie. Havinta go on a tram wiv all them dirty Niracoogurans."

ayePad™

By 'eck it's a bobby dazzler

Yorkshire's toughest tablet computer

When't thee stuck out on't moor in't middle of gale force seven winds, tryin' to deliver lamb in't one 'and and fix brekkin van in t'other, you need a tablet computer what's as tough as thee. T'Apple's letteest **ayePad** is designed specifically for use on't field, down't mine and in seemingly perpetual drizzle. So don't be thee big ole' lummox, get down to **ayeStore** today.

PLUS get owt for nowt

FREE wireless Dingle wi't purchase

Them there t'extra bits:

Now in't choice-a colours

How about this right champion 'andle for't mekkin' ayePad into plasterin' trowel? Perfec for't fixin' side a't barn or sommet'em wonky bricks on't house.

What berra way't fettle 'ole in't back garden than wi't spaaade 'andle attachment? Now thee can surf t'internet whilst gathering 'taters f't supper.

Come'n avva pick at it in't following stores: —

(Leeds)   (Huddersfield)   (Bradford)   (Wakefield)   (Keighley)   t'Apple™

The leading monthly magazine for owners of hate-filled pets

HOSTILE DOG

£2.99

December 2012

Are your dog's eyes beady enough?

"He's normally lovely with kids but…"

Predictable stories of the 'only time' your pet flipped out

How to re-attach an arm - FAST

15
best ways to prise your dog's immensely powerful jaws from a stranger's thigh

FREE INSIDE
A-Z of hostile dog names from Arserender to Zerialkiller

Your problems solved, with Holly Harper

Should I colour in my bald patch with a felt tip?

Dear Holly,

I'm going prematurely bald and I am paranoid that women won't be able to see beyond my massive shiny noggin, glinting in the sunshine. Do you think anyone will notice if I use a sharpie to colour it in? How does Wayne Rooney do it?

Adam, Wiltshire

Dear Simon

A big boy from Y6 has a brother who knows the best friend of a lady who once saw Coleen Rooney on the tube, and he told us that apparently the reason Wayne Rooney was banned for two matches is because he was caught illegally harvesting the hair of corpses in order to fashion his new barnet. Apparently he started out using belly button fluff borrowed from the navels of sex workers, but it just kept sliding off his bonce and making him look daft in Liverpool nightclubs, so he soon escalated to grave robbery. One dark night, when Kai was in bed and Coleen was tanning her earlobes, Wayne dressed in a black football strip and sneaked into the cemetery. By the light of the moon he used a pair of nail scissors to plunder the armpit hair of thirty-seven cadavers, pausing only to vomit into his football boots. But it was all worth it, when he could look in a mirror with pride again and see a man with bizarre fluffy corpse-hair grinning back. Unfortunately, Wayne failed to seek the permission of the head of FIFA in advance and therefore he was immediately branded a bad sport and told he was banned from playing until he had made an even more magnificent toupee for Sepp Blatter.

Hope that helps! Holly x

Your astrological week ahead, with Psychic Bob

Taurus
20 APRIL - 20 MAY
You've made all the necessary work preparations before your holiday – assigning urgent projects to co-workers and informing clients of your absence, etc. Just need to drop that virulent strain of botulism into the water cooler and you're good to go.

Gemini
21 MAY-20 JUN
Sure, you could use that last bit of money to fend off your creditors or you could blow the lot on tasty cocktails with bits of fruit in them. What are they going to do, repossess your vomit?

Cancer
21 JUN-22 JUL
OI! OI! SAVELOY! Sorry, I mean, dearly beloved, we are gathered here today…

Leo
23 JUL-22 AUG
It's called *Avengers Assemble* presumably because 'Chronic Masturbators and Sociopaths Assemble' wouldn't fit on the poster.

Virgo
23 AUG-22 SEP
If you look up the word 'gullible' in the dictionary it will be the first time you've opened a book for at least three years.

Libra
23 SEP-23 OCT
It's amazing The Bangles had such a successful career when they didn't even have the common sense to realise that during a manic Monday, making the bed could wait until they got home.

Scorpio
24 OCT-21 NOV
This week Jupiter drives past your living room window in your car with your wife's head methodically bobbing up and down in his lap. But no, you insisted you could beat him at rock-paper-scissors.

Sagittariu s
22 NOV-21 DEC
You work hard and you pay your taxes but where's the video of your prolonged racist rants on the London underground?

Capricorn
22 DEC-19 JAN
Honesty is usually the best policy, but owning a car in our part of town you may also want to include fire, theft and being driven though an off-licence window.

Aquarius
20 JAN-19 FEB
No word from ITV about your soap pilot following the lives of bright orange farmers called 'Emmerdale Winton'.

Pisces
20 FEB-20 MAR
It's terrible to watch a friend slide slowly into the jaws of alcoholism, especially when you've still got another three days on those poxy antibiotics.

Aries
21 MAR-19 APR
During your road trip across the USA you came across a small, close-knit community of people who smoked furiously and wrote self-referential novels. You'll never forget the simple folk of Amis country.

"Hey Dermot, is that you in there, masturbating?"

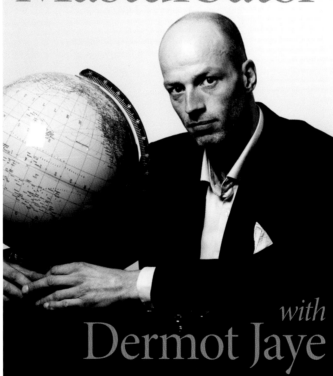

Stylish **Masturbator**

with Dermot Jaye

GUILTY as charged, I hurriedly finished and opened the cubicle door to discover the baritone belonged to my old sparring partner Grayson Stott, CEO of exciting male lifestyle brand D-Lux.

This happened in the rest rooms of Soho media enclave Prick House – the pounding beats of the 2011 Advertorial Awards after-party just barely audible through its high quality Argentinian chestnut doors.

We did not shake hands, partly because my left hand had some semen on it. But also because handsome, towering Ivy Leaguer Grayson was holding, in each of his manly mitts, a giant yellow foam comma.

We exchanged pleasantries, enquired after each others' attractive wives (actually his delightful spouse Tabitha has one nipple 0.4cm higher than the other, a forgivable but significant genetic faux pas I noted during Alain de Botton's session at Hay). It wasn't long before I skilfully steered the conversation to exactly why the fuck he was holding a pair of giant punctuation marks.

"You need an ironic attitude at these boring industry events, right? So I've put myself in inverted commas. While I'm holding these everything I do and say is ironic. My very essence is ironic."

Like the best work of Isaac Newton or Tony Parsons, it was a miracle of innovation that seemed obvious in retrospect. Grayson's porta-commas had made him 100% sincerity-proof.

But … there were flaws.

I asked, pointedly: "So when you just congratulated me on my *Best Advertorial About A Divers' Watch* award, you were being ironic?"

The big lummox was flummoxed: "Uh … I … ah … Dermot … between you and I … I …"

His square jaw fell defeatedly to his chest.

"I … I have no wit."

Later that evening I see Grayson deep in conversation with Kelly Brook, frantically flapping his commas up and down like an semaphorically-incontinent air traffic controller. Americans. Fuck them.

Dermot Jaye is founding editor and masturbator-at-large of Stylish Masturbator magazine.

If it's broke fix it with the thing that broke it

Housing market is pretty much all we have left, admits Cameron

THE government is to boost the housing market because there really isn't anything else to do, it has been confirmed.

David Cameron and Nick Clegg have unveiled a £400m investment to encourage new building and help first-time buyers after realising Britain had long since given up on anything that was not ultimately about houses.

The prime minister said: "This package will help to re-inflate the house price bubble and give mortgages to people who can't really afford them. Unless anyone has any better ideas?

"It's worth remembering that the only reason the British economy seemed successful in the late '90s was because of a house price bubble and mortgages being given to people who couldn't really afford them, so it's not as if we're in uncharted territory.

"This will definitely work."

Nick Clegg added: "We calculated that if you strip the housing sector out of the British economy you're left with some Duchy Originals marmalade and footballers paying for threesomes.

"So until such times as we actually start making things out of metal, we need to support the foundations of our pretend economy with money we don't really have."

Tom Logan, who has never met anyone with a real job, said: "My father's dying words to me were 'make sure you buy a house you can't afford and fill it with stuff you don't need'.

"He also told me not to listen to people who said a career in public relations is shallow and worthless. He was my hero."

Wasps – in November, says everyone

THERE are still wasps, everyone told everyone else this morning.

The unseasonably warm autumn has meant that millions of wasps across Britain are refusing to die, leading to conversations about them.

And now experts are warning that if the mild weather continues it could cause an unprecedented gap between conversations about television programmes.

Professor Henry Brubaker, of the Institute for Studies, said: "Our National Conversation Grid is showing nothing but wasps for at least another 72 hours.

"In Doncaster a man will say how much he is enjoying the new David Attenborough thing, prompting a random passer-by to say 'frozen planet, my giddy arse' and then show him a photo of a really big wasp that they took with their iPhone while they were spending the afternoon in the park.

"In November."

Professor Brubaker also warned that unless the wasps disappear soon it could cause many people to venture into wildly ill-informed conversations about anthropogenic global warming.

He added: "Then, in their confused state, they may stagger blindly into a Daily Telegraph comment thread, where their brain will die within about four seconds."

Tom Logan, from Peterborough, told his workmates: "I'm sitting outside – in November – having a pint and there it was, a bloody great wasp, going about its business without a care in the world.

"In November.

"I nudged my mate Dave, pointed at the wasp and said 'November'. And he looked at it, shook his head and then eventually said 'November'.

"I'll never forget it."

Britain is sick of Attenborough's lies

Business as usual

Rangers launch 'Fuck the Pope' bingo app
Page 41

Reader offer: 2 for 1

Entertain yourself after the demise of civilisation

Page 39

Back as Number 1

Kim Jong Il's death returns Luke Donald to top of PGA Page 39

the dailymash

www.thedailymash.co.uk — DANGEROUS LEVELS OF CLARITY — Monday 2012

Idiot toffs inadvertently end gun culture

URBAN gun culture is officially over after some red trouser-type dickhead waved a fake pistol around.

POLICE stations across the UK have been inundated by youth gang members surrendering their weapons since a wealthy, foppish friend of buttock host organism Pippa Middleton did for guns what Vanilla Ice did for hip hop.

Youth worker Nikki Hollis said: "What self-respecting street kid wants to look like they're a trainee investment banker called Fergus?

"We're driving the 'guns are for toffs' message home with posters showing a fop wearing deck shoes and a jumper tied around his neck with the slogan 'This piece carries a piece.'"

Gang member Tom Logan said: "I've had to stop carrying a gun in case people think I went to one of those schools in a castle where everyone wanks onto a biscuit.

"I'll probably just get a normal job now. I'm kind of grateful to those bell ends, they've broken the cycle of violence through the power of twattery."

Media analyst Emma Bradford said: "This incident confirms the Middleton sisters as the Kardashians for people who buy things in Jack Wills."

But while urban gun crime appears to be finished, toff-on-toff violence has escalated.

Chelsea resident Julian Cook said: "Right now there's a lot of beef – or as we call it 'filet mignon' – between Chelsea and South Ken. It started over an unpaid champagne bill in the Zanzibar Lounge on King's Road.

"The trend is to shoot your toff rival below the waist, the red trousers mean that ambulance crews can't find the wound to staunch it."

There is, finally, a point to her

Men puzzled by porn that you read

This is very intimidating

MALES are deeply confused by a new sort of pornography that is both for women and made of words.

E L James's novel *50 Shades of Grey*, which has smashed paperback sales records, is simultaneously more extreme than men's own sexual fantasies and requires the user to hold it with both hands.

Network engineer Tom Booker said: "I heard the wife going on to her sister about 50 Shades, but thought it couldn't possibly be pornography because there weren't any pictures.

"However I've just found her logged onto an internet chatroom as spank_me_kindly, asking for a master who will take her to the Red Room of Pain, so something's clearly up."

The book, which chronicles the romance between businessman Christian Grey and college graduate Anastasia Steele, has further confused men by having a respectable cover.

Plumber Roy Hobbs said: "It doesn't have the word 'Slutz' on it in neon lettering. I find that quite intimidating."

However copywriter Julian Cook said: "I'm a sophisticated man. I've known books can be sexy ever since I frotted myself raw to chapter five of James Herbert's *The Rats* aged 13.

"But apparently my life partner, who was furious when I bought her crotchless panties for Valentine's Day, now thinks it's really hot to read about virgins signing contracts to be sex slaves.

"I've suggested we do some of that submissive-dominant stuff but she's told me to piss off. I'll never understand women."

Francesca Johnson, Mr Cook's girlfriend, explained: "Sexual subjugation is hugely arousing when practised with a devastatingly handsome multi-millionaire who buys you iPads and Audis, less so with someone who picks his toenails during *CSI: Miami*."

Large Hadron Collider putting family-run particle colliders out of business

MANY small local particle colliders have been forced to close since the opening of Hadron, it has been claimed.

The Tevatron accelerator in Peterborough is the latest in a string of family-owned electromagnetic propulsion facilities to succumb to the so-called 'Hadron effect'.

Tevatron owner Stephen Malley said: "Forty years ago my father built this particle collider with his bare hands, working evenings and weekends while still holding down a day job as a piano tuner.

"People didn't know anything about science back then, but with a little elbow grease he ended up with a pretty good synchrotron capable of accelerating particles up to 980 GeV.

The Tevatron, last of the great steam-powered accelerators

He called her 'Maggie May' after my grandmother.

"I took over about 10 years ago and even though I've added some new valves and a stereo, we just can't generate the 'collision energy' that everyone's been talking about since Hadron came along. One by one our regular customers have all drifted away to Cern.

"We just wanted to give people the sort of friendly, honest particle collision that you don't get with a big corporate accelerator.

"So today I fired up Maggie May for the last time, but I felt so sad I couldn't even get through the preliminary sequence of ionising hydrogen gas without weeping.

He added: "I try not to hate Brian Cox, but it's hard."

Other recently-defunct accelerators include Le Petit Choux Accelerateur near Avignon and the Dudley-based Megatron.

Megatron owner Nikki Hollis said: "When funding dipped post-Hadron we tried to boost visitor numbers with a tea room and 'Happy Atom Play Park', but there was an incident with a four-year-old getting into the main booster and a subsequent small earthquake that got totally blown out of proportion by the local press.

"I actually wrote to Brian Cox but he wouldn't even give us a signed picture.

"What a bastard."

Pandas already drunk

TWO giant pandas were very drunk within 15 minutes of arriving in Scotland, it has emerged.

Tian Tian and Yang Guang are today sleeping off what experts predict will be the first of many hangovers in their purpose built enclosure.

The new stars of Edinburgh Zoo arrived at around 11am yesterday, in time for what local zoologists described as 'a nice wee sharpener'.

Helen Archer, who was at the zoo with her two children, said: "Tian Tian wasn't keen at first, saying they had been travelling for 26 hours and could really do with a nap.

"But the zookeeper was very insistent and kept saying 'have a drink, c'mon have a drink'. It actually became rather menacing.

"Eventually they both said yes to a rum and coke and soon after that you could see the beginnings of a typical Sunday afternoon session."

She added: "We went off to look at the famous hammered penguins and when we came back an hour later Tian Tian was in the middle of this horrible rant about 'all they fuckin' English pandas'.

"I don't care for the foul language but still, they're a nice distraction from the steady collapse of western society."

Meanwhile, the zoo said it was also hoping the pair will become the first pandas in captivity to hate each other because of religion.

'We would prefer a vodka and lemonade'

Independent Scotland could be exactly the same, warn experts

INDEPENDENCE could leave Scotland exactly the same in every way, experts warned last night.

As Scottish first minister Alex Salmond set out his timetable for an independence referendum, he was dealt a devastating blow after research showed separation from the UK would make absolutely no difference whatsoever.

Professor Henry Brubaker, of the Institute for Studies, said: "It will still be damp, windy and miles from everywhere.

"The Scottish people will continue to shop, drink, complain, work for the council, eat beige food and hate each other because of football, religion or some bastard hybrid of the two.

"They will watch the same television programmes as they did before, mainly because they have all seen Scottish television programmes and they're not making that mistake again.

"They will also retain their baffling sense of er,   and the government will still interfere constantly in people's lives. The only thing that will change is that they'll be reduced to one set of shitwit politicians on which to pin the blame."

Brubaker added: "Meanwhile, the rest of the UK will also remain exactly the same, only more so."

The Scottish National Party condemned the research as racist stereotyping and then welcomed it for proving that independence would be completely risk-free.

The SNP wants to stage the referendum in autumn 2014 while the UK government insists it should take place next year paving the way for an argument so tedious that even a drunk Scotsman would find it difficult to sustain.

It has also emerged that Salmond ditched his initial plan for a referendum on the 700th anniversary of Scotland's victory over England at the Battle of Bannockburn after someone pointed out that it was pathetic.

Leisure time will be spent drumming in the dark

UK 'will return to Stone Age by 2014'

BRITAIN will be a prehistoric barter economy within two years, the Bank of England has predicted.

The bank's latest projections show that negative growth and the collapse of the eurozone will create an economic system based on flint axes, chickens and shiny stones.

Bank of England governor Mervyn King said: "By 2014 job and mortgage worries will be replaced by concerns about fighting rival tribes with spears.

"And you're not going to have time to update your Facebook status when a wolf has just stolen your baby."

Technology shares plummeted following the announcement. However, traders reported a buoyant market in bear pelts.

Chicken farmer Joseph Turner was upbeat about the collapse of society into violent, brutish chaos.

He said: "I've got 200,000 scabrous hens packed into my stinking warehouses, so basically I'm going to be one of the richest men in England.

"I'll probably marry Liz Hurley and become King of Worcestershire."

Unemployed builder Norman Steele agreed: "I'm six foot four and pretty tasty in a fight, so I'm looking forward to the day when social status is determined by brute force.

"Then I will kill all clever people except the ones that make beer."

Despite the gloomy predictions, King anticipates an improvement in the financial situation by 2050, with the introduction of gold coins and feudalism.

North Korea to execute Kim Jong Il's heart attack

KIM Jong-Il's fatal heart attack is to be executed by firing squad, it has been confirmed.

North Korea's gas-powered state TV channel announced to the four people with televisions that the myocardial infarction was apprehended 'within hours' by the world's best police force and charged with high treason.

A spokesman said: "After stopping the heart of the world's greatest flamenco dancer and inventor of the Beatles it tried to escape down the finest trouser leg in the history of universe.

"With the invaluable help of the ghost of the Dear Leader, our invincible policemen chased it into an alley where it surrendered, burst into tears and then urinated on itself like an American cowboy homosexual."

Paying tribute to Kim's ghost, the spokesman added: "All the scientists who have ever lived say it is the most amazing ghost there will ever be. All other ghosts must commit suicide."

The blockage of the coronary artery will now be tortured, tried and executed in accordance with Kim's wishes.

The spokesman said: "It will be made to sing a song called Kim Jong-Il's Gigantic Sex Organ Makes All Women Hungry for Him and then it will be shot with 9,000 bullets shaped like the Dear Leader's incredible head."

Luke Donald now returns to the top of the PGA rankings if you do not include ghosts

For Christ's sake just teach them, parents tell schools

PARENTS last night asked schools if there was any chance they could, for the love of God, just teach their children.

As it emerged that exam bodies were helping teachers to make exams even easier, parents across the country urged their local school to draw up a list of useful information and then attempt to impart that to their offspring.

Tom Logan, from Hatfield, said: "Reading, writing and a bit of maths. They can get the rest of it from the Discovery Channel.

"Teach them to read and write a proper English sentence. Some angles, maybe an equation here and there. Perhaps a basic understanding of compound interest. Is that too much to fucking ask?

"But please, I beg you, you have to stop all this dicking about. If they fail they fail, but at least you tried to just fucking teach them."

Emma Bradford, from Doncaster, said: "I'd throw in some geography and a bit of science, but most of all – most of all – I want you to stop turning education into some fucking numbers game and in the name of Jesus fucking Christ on a tricycle, just teach my fucking kids some fucking stuff."

A spokesman for the National Union of Teachers said: "Britain needs to decide, once and for all, whether it wants a system that educates children or a system that appears to educate to children.

"Because at the moment we're getting mixed signals."

Logan added: "I have never expressed even the slightest interest in a system that does anything other than educate children.

"In fact, here's a quick lesson – what's the difference between a teacher and an MP? One is an overpaid, over-holidayed, arse-covering piece of shit and so is the other one."

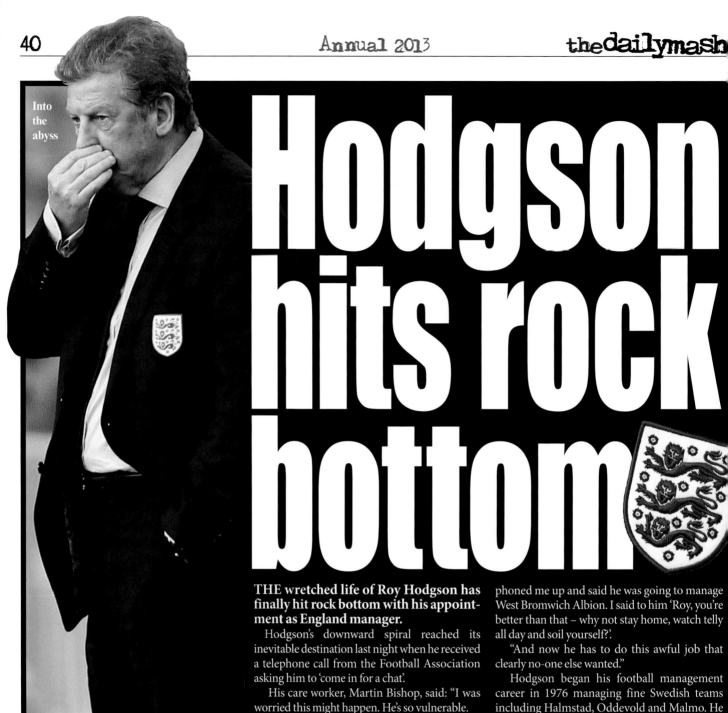

Into the abyss

Hodgson hits rock bottom

THE wretched life of Roy Hodgson has finally hit rock bottom with his appointment as England manager.

Hodgson's downward spiral reached its inevitable destination last night when he received a telephone call from the Football Association asking him to 'come in for a chat'.

His care worker, Martin Bishop, said: "I was worried this might happen. He's so vulnerable.

"I suppose the alarm bells started ringing when he became manager of Liverpool. I tried to get him a job in the McDonalds on the high street but they said they'd had a few bad experiences with Liverpool managers.

"Apparently Graeme Souness used to pelt the customers with frozen baps.

"Anyway, I stood by him until one day he phoned me up and said he was going to manage West Bromwich Albion. I said to him 'Roy, you're better than that – why not stay home, watch telly all day and soil yourself?'.

"And now he has to do this awful job that clearly no-one else wanted."

Hodgson began his football management career in 1976 managing fine Swedish teams including Halmstad, Oddevold and Malmo. He even managed Inter Milan twice, but after a severe blow to the head his faculties became impaired and he signed a contract with Fulham.

Bishop added: "That was the beginning of the end. Since then it has been a steady descent, each job more demeaning than the last.

"He used to live in Switzerland you know. It's such a shame."

Irishman hot favourite to b[e]

The Gold Cup goes to whoever pushes this little chap off Kauto Star

MARTIN O'Hanlon, a 38 year-old from Kerry, is the bookies' choic[e] for champion drinker at the Chel[-] tenham Festival.

The four-day sauce-neckin[g] event, which takes place next t[o] some horses at Cheltenham race[-] course, attracts top professiona[l] drinkers from around the world.

This year's 5-6 favourite is garru[-] lous Irishman O'Hanlon, who wil[l] be coming over on the ferry wit[h] four grand in his top pocket and

Some people not into football

A SMALL number of English people are not responding correctly to football, it has emerged.

The Institute for Studies believes it has identified a sub-group of the English race that is not only indifferent to football, but in some cases actively dislikes the game.

Professor Henry Brubaker said: 'What's truly shocking is that some of these individuals are male. It had long been accepted that some women and homosexuals struggle to engage with football, but it's harder to understand how a straight man might malfunction in this way.

"We have government approval to carry out necessary tests on the 'ball-deniers'. Since vivisecting several of them and looking at bits of their brains under a microscope, they are biologically identical to fully-functioning humans.

"Some of our experiments may be considered inhumane but clearly we cannot risk whatever is wrong with them mutating into a virus."

The phenomenon of ball-deniers became apparent last week when Roy Hobbs passed through his village summoning all males to the England game.

Self-appointed football-summoner Hobbs said: "Before each game I travel the streets in my shiny official England cloak, knocking on each door in turn so that all males of football age know it is time to attend the pub."

He is more human than them

However 36-year-old Wayne Hayes failed to respond appropriately.

Hobbs said: "He refused to join us. Looking over his shoulder, I could see that his television was switched to a non-sport channel. I didn't understand."

Hayes, who has since been quarantined in the Institute for Studies' laboratory, said: "I don't know what it is, I just struggle to identify emotionally with these men and their leather sphere.

"Perhaps it's because I've never met any of the players in 'England'. They feel like strangers to me.

"Please take these electrodes out of my nose, I think they're touching my brain. Is my family safe?"

Professor Brubaker said: "Hayes claims to be naturally ambivalent to football. Clearly this is impossible. On some level, even if he doesn't realise it, he's being spiteful."

Rangers pledges sectarianism as usual

MURDEROUS chant enabler Rangers last night pledged financial meltdown will not interfere with all the hating.

Going into administration could cost the Glasgow giants 10 points in the Scottish 'Premier' League, putting them within 25 points of everyone apart from Celtic, but the club urged fans to remain positive and continue thinking up new rhymes for 'Ratzinger'.

A spokesman said: "As long as there's a Rangers, there will always be one half of Glasgow wishing the other half dead. Everyone should carry on with their sectarian grudges and post-match domestic abuse as normal."

The club faces a potentially fatal £49m tax bill while season ticket sales have dropped since a ban on singing songs about being 'up to one's knees in Fenian blood'.

Now Rangers officials are to meet with UK Jihad 'tsar' Abu Qatada to discuss new ways of making religious hatred more revenue dynamic.

Ideas include blackmailing priests, Fuck the Pope Bingo and an iPhone app that can identify Catholics by measuring the width of their skulls.

Meanwhile, Celtic fans have set up a Rangers rescue fund after realising that without their Old Firm rivals their lives would be utterly hollow. Celtic fan Bill McKay said: "You've seen the football. No-one is coming here for the football."

The Rangers spokesman added: "It would be very easy to play the blame game, but the unavoidable truth is that the inland revenue is now a wholly-owned subsidiary of Opus Dei."

The club also pledged to continue buying carpet-baggers who couldn't hack it in a proper league and getting its arse handed to it in Europe by teams with names like Vlodzy Kravnaj.

They could try waving this really, really hard

drunkest person at Cheltenham

'virtually unlimited' capacity for rum and coke.

O'Hanlon's trainer, Stephen Malley, said: "Martin romped home last weekend at Kelso, consuming 194 units of alcohol over a 48-hour stretch. That includes 98 units before he had his first piss.

"He's a great competitor and a fantastic personality. The crowd loves it when he doesn't seem that pissed but then tries to leave the bar via an imaginary door."

Earlier this season O' Hanlon, who stands 13 hands high when upright, sustained a serious injury to his drinking arm when he repeatedly punched a road sign following a mid-week session at Doncaster.

Malley said: "Luckily he was still able to grab people round the neck and force them to sing *Wild Colonial Boy*."

Drinkers' rights groups have called for the event to be banned after last year's favourite, the popular Scot Davey McBride, stumbled into a roadside ditch and had to be shot.

But a spokesman for the organisers said: "The drinkers love it. You can see the enjoyment in their eyes and to stop them doing it would be going against nature.

"Unfortunately, when they fall over they're often too drunk to tell us if they're okay and so we have to put them down."

the dailymash

www.thedailymash.co.uk   **PERSECUTE THE INTELLIGENT**   Monday 2012

WOMEN WRONG

SAYS CLEVEREST PERSON IN WORLD

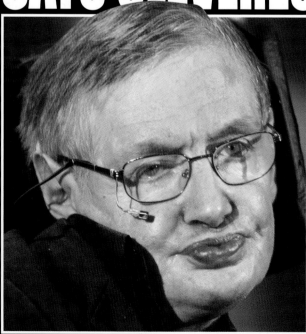

Deals only in scientific fact

THE fundamental wrongness of women has been established beyond doubt. Professor Stephen Hawking, the world's cleverest human since 1988, has confirmed that women are not only wrong but probably stupid as well.

In an interview with New Scientist, Professor Hawking said: "Have you tried having a grown-up conversation with one of them? Fucking hell.

"They are wrong. And I know everything there is to know about the universe, so that's that."

Tom Logan, from Hatfield, backed Professor Hawking's theory, adding: "I also really liked the way he described them as 'constantly expanding and contracting' and 'infinitely dense.'"

But Logan's girlfriend, Helen Archer, insisted: "He didn't say any of that.

"All he said was that women are a 'complete mystery'. Which is actually rather romantic and makes me think of myself as a beautiful star that no-one has ever really taken the time to try and understand."

Logan stressed: "Saying something is a complete mystery is exactly the same as saying that it is wrong about everything all the time. As you well know.

"But let's abandon Professor Hawking's years of study and continue to live in your alternate universe where the laws of physics state that you're the only one who can remember exactly what people said and the tone in which they said it."

Archer continued: "In your universe the laws of physics state that all women are wrong except your fucking mother.

"Also, no disrespect to Professor Hawking, but you can't really tell if he's being ironic or not."

Logan added: "Cleverest. Person. In. World."

SMOOTHIES CONTAIN DANGEROUS LEVELS OF PR BULLSHIT

You will drink it then you will piss it out

THE amount of drivel on smoothie bottles could affect consumers' mental health, it has been claimed.

Research by the Institute for Studies found that smoothie packaging contains an average 50bsgrams – the unit of measurement used to assess bullshit – exceeding government guidelines.

Professor Henry Brubaker said: "Smoothie makers plaster their products with glib crud about 'love and hugs', 'meanie-free deliciousness', 'more refreshing than a box of monkeys', that sort of crap.

"Usually it's written in an nauseatingly pseudo-casual tone designed to evoke a sense of 'matey-ness'.

"When bullshit exceeds a certain level, it has a very specific effect on the human brain, causing feelings of severe agitation and annoyance."

Last year doctors identified a condition dubbed smoothiephrenia, where smoothie-makers' ingratiating tripe triggers a psychotic state.

Professor Brubaker said: "A 38-year-old man called Roy Hobbs drove a stolen bus into the London offices of Organojoy Smoothies, whose slogan was 'Full of win'.

"He then killed himself by repeatedly head-butting a wall until his frontal lobe caved in. His wife said he'd read the phrase 'yum alert' on a smoothie bottle and just wanted it out of his brain.

"Smoothie makers need to stop riding around their offices on scooters and start taking responsibility for the amount of psychic damage they're doing.

"They must realise that consumers don't want a relationship with them. They just want to metabolise the drink and go about their day.

"This also applies to people who make pies that come in little boxes."

CAMERON PUNCHES A TRAMP

David Cameron rounded off his spirited performance in the Commons yesterday by smacking a vagrant in the throat.

After asking Dennis Skinner to die and telling Margaret Hodge that she looked like an old man, the prime minister stormed out of the Palace of Westminster and assaulted the first available tramp.

Tory backbencher, Martin Bishop, said: "He ran over to this thin, shabby looking person and just went absolutely fucking mental on him while shouting 'point of order! point of order!' in a manic, high-pitched voice.

"George Osborne was sobbing and telling him to stop but he wouldn't listen and just kept raining light slaps on the homeless chap's face until he was exhausted."

Downing Street has now asked the Speaker if Prime Minister's Questions can be renamed 'The Prime Minister Calls You an Arse' while all official statements from Mr Cameron's office will now begin with 'Listen, fuckface'.

Earlier Mr Cameron told Labour leader Ed Miliband that he will order an enquiry into Jeremy Hunt's relationship with News Corporation 'just after I've finished doing your missus'.

Bishop added: "It's not that I'm worried the government is struggling to regain its authority, it's that the prime minister seems to be having a nervous breakdown."

A Downing Street spokesman said: "The prime minister will continue to have a nervous breakdown in order to maintain Britain's cherished triple-A credit rating."

Women offered chance to give birth anally

Men may finally be of some use during labour

WOMEN in the UK will soon have the option to give birth anally, as part of the NHS reform bill.

The new rules, which come into effect in early March 2012, have been introduced to make the whole process of childbirth a more pleasurable experience for women, according to health experts.

Dr David Stark of UK Healthcare Trust: "It makes sense to combine the joy of defecation with the rather more uncomfortable act of giving birth to a human.

"I am sick to death of women moaning on and on about the agony of childbirth and their gaping, flaccid vaginas. We hope the new procedure will put an end to this hormonal nonsense."

Under the new rules, when women discover they are pregnant, they can make a choice between a traditional vaginal birth, a Caesarean section or an anal birth. It is expected that most women, including celebrities like Victoria Beckham and Angelina Jolie, will jump at the chance to have a 'rectal child' and keep their clitorae intact.

An NHS spokesman said: "Several key changes will occur on labour wards. Instead of midwives, there'll just be immigrant toilet attendants with minimal English language skills who sign a laminated cleaning rota every 20 minutes and watch the soap dispenser like a hawk.

"And mothers will not be offered epidurals, they'll just be handed a copy of The Times' crossword and left to get on with it.

"In addition, there'll be much less waiting around for labour to start, as women will be given a strong cup of coffee and a cigarette. And there'll be no more screams of agony. All you'll hear are sighs of pleasure."

Jackie Spencer, a professional feminist from Peterborough, said: "Women should re-claim the back passage as our own and make it all pretty with ribbons and bows and things."

Fuel shortage caused by warning of fuel shortage

GOVERNMENT warnings of a fuel shortage have proved to be uncannily accurate.

Within hours of Francis Maude telling everyone to put a gun turret on their garage, petrol stations reported long queues of terrified people offering their children in exchange for a fill-up.

Mr Maude said: "I got a right load of shit from everyone yesterday but it turns out I was absolutely spot on.

"But will they apologise? Will they fuck."

The cabinet office minister admitted his fuel shortage prediction was based on an educated guess, but denied strongly that it was a fluke.

He added: "Watch this.

"I think there's going to be a milk shortage."

Mr Maude was then forced to dive out of the way as four million people stampeded towards the nearest Asda, stripping it of milk as if it was a goat in a piranha tank.

As the dust settled, Mr Maude continued: "It's weird isn't it? It's like I'm totally in the 'zone'.

"Let's try it with pasties."

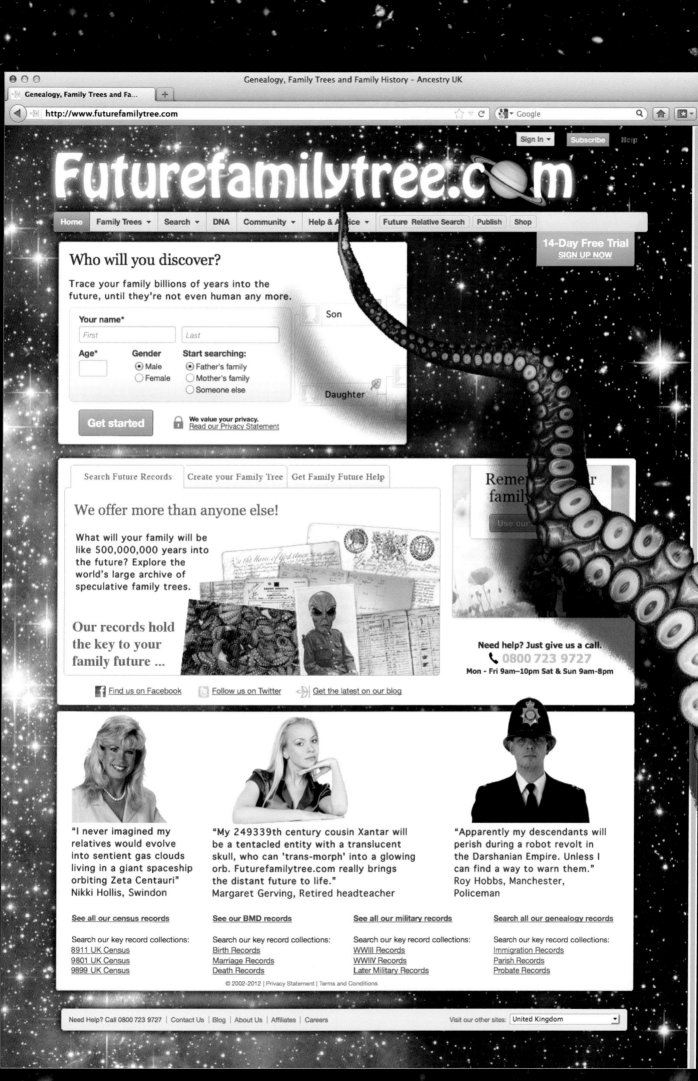

Dr Julian Cook's Science Laboratory

'WE HAVE ALL BEEN INTERFERED WITH'

ALTHOUGH I am a man of science, I have a lot of time for Cardinal Keith O'Brien. This is because he has much in common with the Higgs Boson, whose responsibilities also include giving mass and wrangling with flouncy little pests who want to combine with each other in extravagant partnership ceremonies.

Cardinal O'Brien, like the Higgs, is an almighty mass giving enigma. Ordinary people are unpredictable little quarks who tear around the universe without a clue what they're doing. As mass ceremonies are difficult to avoid, all quarks at some point will end up in one. Some will escape unfazed by the experience and will continue rattling along at light speed to somewhere like Alicante or Mecca. But others will be rendered heavy, sluggish and will be made to do things they wouldn't normally have done. Any massive particle – be it me, an aubergine, an altar boy – we've all been interfered with.

Cardinal O'Brien is annoyed because he believes David Cameron is trying to redefine reality. Indeed, redefining reality is very dangerous and I can fully understand his concerns. You see usually, quarks hook up in combinations of one quark and one antiquark. This is the way the cardinal likes it because it's nice and simple. Sometimes, three drunk quarks hook up to make a baryon – the cardinal can live with this even if it does make him a big fidgety. Some fantasists say you can even get them with five but thus far, they've been unable to back this up with authentic footage so it's safe to assume they're liars.

The Cardinal's right: you don't want to mess around with reality. And if you must repeatedly participate in risky, high-energy collisions with lots of like-minded quarks, you better make sure you do it in a controlled environment, preferably somewhere secret and underground on mainland Europe – the way Professor Brian Cox does. It's demoralising to see all your particles running off to form mind-boggling unions with each other. But in time I think Cardinal O'Brien will find there's nothing to worry about. I have several catholic colleagues and, for the moment at least, it seems none of them are prepared to leave their wives and have a gay marriage bash in the local chapel. And even if they did, they all have such fabulous singing voices and are such lovely dancers, that it really would be a thoroughly jolly knees-up.

Dr Julian Cook is a research fellow at the Institute for Studies

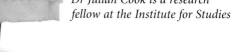

Quark on quark collisions are grotesque

The perfect mentally-unhinged macaron recipe

HAVE you noticed how macarons are the sweet craze now that cupcakes have suddenly become social poison?

It's normal to give them individual names

Ingredients:
- 140g/5oz ground almonds
- 25g/1oz bodily fluids of your choice
- 275g/9¾oz icing sugar
- Clump of your hair
- 4 free-range egg whites
- Twigs

For the filling:
- 75ml/2½fl oz whipping cream
- 75g/2½oz gin
- 75g/2½oz mascarpone cheese
- More gin
- 25g/1oz icing sugar
- Yet more gin

Preparation:
- Preheat the oven to 170/C/325F/Gas 5 and line a large baking tray with baking paper while ignoring the voices in your head telling you to do things with scissors.

- Put the icing sugar, ground almonds and 40g/1½oz egg whites together in a large bowl and mix with intense aggression repeating the phrase 'Biscuits, I'll give them fucking biscuits'.

- Put the water and caster sugar in a small pan and heat gently to melt the sugar, then turn up the heat and boil, boil, boil, boil until the mixture appears to be screaming 'no more'. Then give it more. Make it suffer.

- Whisk the remaining 50g/2oz egg whites in a small bowl until medium-stiff, then abandon everything temporarily while you run upstairs and have a cry. Return to kitchen, repeatedly slap own face while saying 'we can do this, it's all fine'.

- Spoon into the piping bag. With the bag held vertically, pipe the words HELP ME, twisting the bag after each letter (biscuits are usually round but it's OK, you don't have to do what THEY say any more and that includes the doctors).

- Leave to stand for 30 minutes to form a skin then bake in the oven for 12–15 minutes with the door slightly ajar until firm. Remove from the oven, lift the paper off the baking tray and leave the macaron to cool on the paper. Write note along lines of 'I hope you love these like you could never love me. I'll always remember Tuscany'.

- Insert head into oven.

- Hope someone comes (if no one does, the biscuits will stay fresh for up to two days).

CAT'S ENTERTAINMENT

A feline perspective on the latest cinema releases

with tabby **Martin Harper**

I've been trying to get into Prometheus (15) for weeks but the cleaners keep chasing me out. I bet Peter Bradshaw doesn't get harangued out of screenings by an overweight woman with a hare lip and a broom.

Anyway I finally had success this week after nine hours of waiting by the screen door, purring. The film itself is quite confusing. Something about Noomi Rapace getting spayed with a lazer coupled with some musings on the origins of mankind, which it's hard to care about when you're a cat.

I found a pair of discarded 3D glasses on the floor but they were much wider than my head so I could only look through one lens at a time, which didn't seem to have the desired effect.

I went to sleep twice although I don't count that against the film because I like sleeping.

There's another film out called Fast Girls (12A) about some human females that like to run EVEN THOUGH THEY ARE NOT BEING CHASED. Sorry, but just running for no reason could cause a nearby dog's prey drive to kick in. Then it would chase the girls and, if they couldn't get on a fence, tear them to shreds. The main characters in Fast Girls do not get savaged by terriers but they should for being so stupid.

Another issue, less directly related to the film, is that I couldn't get into my seat because I wasn't heavy enough to pull the bottom bit down. I had to dangle off it, swinging back and forth, until it gradually lowered. Then when I hopped up it slammed shut like a damn Venus flytrap.

Sorry my problem I know but it's hard to focus the critical eye when you're being eaten by a chair.

SQUID MONSTER ATTACK

"You can't let a bit of monster-based carnage stop you celebrating the queen"

MILLIONS of Britons turned out for the Queen's four-day celebrations undaunted by the 500-foot mutant squid that was destroying London.

Huge crowds of well-wishers lined the banks of the Thames on Sunday to watch a spectacular flotilla, continuing to cheer and wave even as tentacles thicker than tree trunks emerged from the water, seizing boats and smashing them against each other.

The Queen and Prince Philip waved and

Royals back at their shit office jobs

MEMBERS of the royal family are gutted to be back at their desks after a four-day break, it has emerged.

After a bumper four-day weekend of celebrations and boozing the British monarchy, who have to do normal shit jobs to make ends meet, have returned to normality with a bump.

Prince Charles is a sales ledger clerk for a building supplies firm in Gloucester.

He said: "I've got arseloads of emails to delete and a banging headache from all the grog.

"It was a great weekend but I'm wondering whether it was all worth it, I'm really rough today.

"I wish I didn't have to be here but I've got two kids, no pension and a girlfriend who spends all my money on hats.

"Ideally being a prince would be something one could do full-time, although I'm not sure exactly how that would work.

Meanwhile Princess Anne is back at work as a receptionist at Fitness First in Cheltenham.

She said: "The juice dispenser's broken and we've run out of large towels. It's absolutely typical of when I have a couple of days off, everything goes to pot.

"Also I feel horrific and have just had a proper full-on white in the disabled toilets

DOESN'T STOP JUBILEE FUN

miled, undaunted as a vast gelatinous shape hauled itself from the belly of the river, tossing tentaclefuls of screaming bystanders into its beaked maw.

Mayor of London Boris Johnson said: "It appears that the large number of boats disturbed a skyscraper-sized carnivore, probably some type of squid that had been mutated by the vast amounts of human filth pumped into the Thames.

"But even an estimated 1,500,000 fatalities couldn't dampen the indomitable British spirit."

Families waved flags even as they ran screaming with buildings crashing to the ground around them.

52-year-old Roy Hobbs said: "You can't let a bit of monster-based carnage stop you celebrating the Queen. Also now that most people are dead or dying I've got a much better view of the procession."

Mother-of-two Emma Bradford was in the crowd on Tuesday at Buckingham Palace, where the Queen and family members waved from the balcony against a backdrop of a city aflame. Behind them in the sky, fighter jets and surface-to-air missiles could be seen engaging the creature.

Emma Bradford said: "It's been a lovely weekend. I've got some of the creature's acid saliva on me which has slightly melted my left arm, but I can still wave a flag with my right.

"You could hear the Queen just fine above the explosions and the monster's weird cries of agonised rage, saying what a nice time she was having."

Royal biographer Nikki Hollis said: "It's just a shame BBC coverage of the event focused on people being eaten rather than capturing the true spirit of Britain."

He's off to the abattoir next week

Britain pathetically excited about sunshine

Angry motorist threatening to use mobile on forecourt

A CRAZED motorist is brandishing a mobile phone on a garage forecourt, it has emerged.

As the petrol crisis deepens, 38-year-old sales manager Roy Hobbs has been cordoned off by the military as he threatens to press the green 'call' button on his iPhone 3, which would trigger the vague but dreadful Thing That Happens When You Use Your Phone at a Garage.

It is believe that marksmen are in place on the roof of a nearby Toys 'R' Us, with instructions to shoot the father-of-two in the head if he moves to operate the phone.

Technologist Nikki Hollis said: "While it is not altogether clear why one must not use a mobile at a garage – no one has ever done it – we are fairly sure the result involves a crater, possibly also massive carnivorous slug things issuing from the bowels of the earth, like in the evergreen Kevin Bacon film *Tremors*.

"Texting is fine though, it's just voice calls that are the problem."

Hobbs shouted: "I'm just an ordinary man who's had enough. Don't think I won't do this.

"In case my kids are watching this on television, daddy loves you and one day you'll understand."

He added: "I just want some petrol and a disappointing savoury pastry, that's all. Those twin pedestals on which this nation stands.

"Although while we're on the subject, how can the staff at this garage claim they 'don't have a toilet'? Presumably they shit in some bushes, like badgers."

THE prospect of decent weather has inspired truly heartbreaking levels of joy across the UK.

As forecasters predicted temperatures bordering on the pleasant with tolerable amounts of rain, Britons were scampering in circles like over-enthusiastic termites, hardly knowing what to do with themselves.

Office worker Tom Logan said: It's going to be hot and sunny! Not just hot or sunny, but both at the same time.

"I'm going to eat my lunch outside with my sleeves rolled up to my elbows. And you can't get much better than that.

"Everything's going to be alright forever."

Sales co-ordinator Emma Bradford said: "I've bought a straw hat and a Summer Fruits Oasis in anticipation of the first beam of sunlight penetrating the dense wall of grey cloud.

"Let me just check out the window ... nothing yet. But it's coming. It's coming."

The prospect of several hours of pleasantness has already inspired gloating headlines about how it's going to be 'hotter than the Meditteranean'.

Montenegro resident Alexander Vrbensky said: "My British cousin called me about it, I had to pretend to be angry, like 'oh no, I'm so jealous, grrr I wish I lived with you in Swindon, when can I get a flight?'

"Then I went to the beach with a group of beautiful girls and ate large fruits, same as every day."

  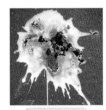

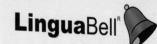

Increasingly debauched jubilee celebrations enter second week

BRITAIN has been warned to wind down its jubilee partying, with many celebrants now having been seven nights without sleep.

Hordes of desperate glassy-eyed revellers in filthy Union Jack hats still line the Mall, convulsively waving flags as they continue to ingest alcohol and drugs.

Lionel Richie, now naked except for a Weetabix box jammed on his head, has been performing a cappella rave anthems on a makeshift stage while the Red Arrows, most of whom can barely stand, are preparing to fly through the British Museum for their own twisted amusement.

A government spokesman said: "It's time for everyone to go home. Seriously, before we get the army out.

"Admittedly when you tell a nation of mostly-unemployed drunkards it's going to be 'the best party ever' you might expect it to get a little rowdy. But I've just seen Rolf Harris being cooked on a spit by a group of children in Kate Middleton masks."

Although their camera crew left days ago, a gurning Fearne Cotton and Lenny Henry are still narrating events as they unfold, occasionally pausing to interview each other about what it would be like if you could peel back the sky and see the inner workings of the universe.

Royal fan Donna Sheridan said: "I'm not ready to go home yet! It's fucking banging here.

"I've just had a shit in a bin."

Bez has arrived with his best maracas

Right-wing people smart enough to hate everyone

RIGHT-wingers are intelligent enough to know that everyone is ultimately a self-serving bastard, according to new research.

The Institute for Studies found that while stupidity leads to racism, right wingers were more likely to know not to stand in front of George Monbiot at the top of some stairs.

The research also showed that Thatcherites can be interested in quantum physics, while Labour voters include barely sentient fist-throwers like John Prescott and Cheryl Cole.

Professor Henry Brubaker said: "Deciding who's cleverest between left and right is like deciding which tube of Smarties would make the best Pope.

"On one side you have people who think capitalism is a great idea but hasn't been done properly yet and on the other you have people who think the forced redistribution of wealth is a great idea but hasn't been done properly yet. It's not exactly a Mensa toga party.

"But right wingers are at least intelligent enough to assume that everyone is a potential enemy. Especially those who give hugs instead of handshakes.

"And while racism, homo-phobia and insisting climatology is a pyramid sales scam are all a bit dense, so is standing on top of a pile of skulls and shouting, 'let's try it again.'"

But Julian Cook, from Finsbury Park, insisted that, if you thought about it, Stalin was actually right wing, which everyone on the left thought was a very clever thing to say.

He continued: "Socialism will always work brilliantly because it is humanity's natural instinct."

Roy Hobbs, from Guildford, added: "What a poof."

Take Me Out contestants shot dead after escape from holding pen

Manford has blood on his hands

THIRTY-FOUR participants in television rutting event *Take Me Out* have been killed by ITV rangers after escaping from their secure backstage enclosure.

ITV insiders claim the sexually-voracious humanoids – genetically engineered by the channel to appear in its light entertainment shows – escaped after chewing through the titanium bars of their cage.

A source said: "This was bound to happen. The male and female enclosures were too close together, they would smell each other and get worked up into a frenzy.

"We usually have Jason Manford backstage to keep them quiet with some material about sat navs with funny voices, but last night he got stuck on the motorway."

He continued: "The females were out first,

killing the guard then rutting with his mauled corpse. Shots were fired, and alpha female Geordayna fell dead.

"With their leader down the rest of the females fled through the fire exit, clambering over cars as they disappeared into nearby woods.

"Enraged by the loss of their potential mates, the males were banging the sides of their cage, hooting and hurling faeces.

"Their leader Big D aka the D-Man, instantly recognisable by his funky hair, partly see-through shirt and highly defined abdominal muscles, grabbed a keeper in a headlock and

took his cage keys.

"Most of the males were soon recaptured with the aid of electro-prods and pornography. But a small group led by Big D and his friend 'Quiffster' left the building.

"Helicopter teams containing ITV rangers were scrambled, putting the creatures down with head shots. Big D was killed while having sex with a swan in the middle of the M5.

"It's what he would have been wanted."

Take Me Out is hosted by Paddy McGuinness, who was still a schoolboy when he was discovered by ITV scouts throwing smaller children's bags onto the roof of the science block.

PRINCE WILLIAM DESPERATE FOR THREESOME

THE Duke of Cambridge's '30 things to do before you're 30' list gives him less than 24 hours to have a threesome, it has emerged.

William, who celebrates his 30th birthday on Thursday, initially tried to persuade his wife of one year to get it on with him and Cheryl Cole as part of the Diamond Jubilee celebrations earlier this month, but was firmly rebuffed.

A subsequent Royal decree ordering Jordan and 'the blonde one off Countdown' to meet the prince behind a Buckingham Palace sentry box was cancelled after Kate Mid-

dleton saw plans for a souvenir plate designed to commemorate the encounter.

The Prince has eliminated all the other things on his list, including driving a convertible, sleeping with a friend's girl-friend and losing £10,000 at roulette, which he did to amuse schoolfriends on his eighth birthday.

He said: "I got lost in a country where I don't understand a word the natives say when I visited Glasgow, I was arrested for being drunk in charge of a Sea King helicopter in the

Falklands, and I killed a man just to watch him die during my gap year in Chile.

"I can't really do the one about quitting your job without dying, so I fired my equerry instead. But I've only got one day to get dual action under my belt without Kate finding out and I don't think I'm going to do it."

On hearing of his brother's plight, Prince Harry ordered that the eight-volume Order of the Garter's Register of Dirty Girls be brought from St George's Chapel, Windsor.

BT couple's son to kill housemate with pitchfork

THE storyline of the latest BT adverts will follow the previous couple's son as he spirals into a pit of murderous drug-fuelled sexual obsession.

In the forthcoming commercials Joe, teenage son of the older woman who hooked up with the scarecrow-ish dick from *My Family*, leaves home and falls into a deadly broadband-based love triangle.

Mentally unhinged by the awfulness of his parents, first-year student Joe becomes obsessed with beautiful housemate Anna. He secretly installs webcams in her bedroom, watching her undress via his super-fast BT broadband connection.

The plot takes a violent turn when Joe returns home following a four-day crystal meth bender to find Anna kissing floppy-haired fellow housemate and love rival Simon.

Without saying a word, the glassy-eyed fresher goes calmly to his room and returns with a pitchfork, plunging it into Simon's chest while repeatedly screaming 'now you are mine, now you are mine, temptress whore'.

Subsequent adverts will follow Joe as he uses BT Infinity broadband internet to stalk terrified Anna, who flees to Tangier.

A BT spokesman said: "Customer feedback about the previous slew of adverts said people wanted more impalement and suffering.

"As a bonus we also get to see Joe masturbating furiously on a fire escape, while crying."

Jeremy Sports had a vision

Ailing JJB targets people who do sport

TROUBLED sloth-wear vendor JJB Sports is to market its goods at sporty people.

Since its formation in 1971, JJB has built a nationwide network of stores servicing the tracksuit needs of idle people and petty criminals.

However recent changes to the benefits system and a clampdown on the sort of thefts where the loot is taken straight to a cash-exchange shop have eroded its core customer base.

A JJB spokesman said: "The idea came during a crisis meeting when an executive asked where the word 'sports' in JJB Sports came from.

"It's actually the surname of Jeremy John Brian Sports, the chain's beloved, long-deceased founder who designed the original 'tracksuit bottoms'.

"Back in the 70s television channels were called 'tracks', hence 'tracksuit' was the name Mr Sports gave to his lightweight television-watching trousers.

"But by pure coincidence, the type of breathable, shiny leisure-cum-burglary-wear we sell is quite well-suited to sports like running or tennis."

He added: "The new message is, our clothes aren't just great for telly, robbing or sitting outside Wetherspoons smoking skunk while repeatedly pulling your terrier's lead so hard its front legs leave the ground. You can do sport in them.

"Our only problem now is that no-one except middle class children or retired dentists really does any physical activity."

Banksy defaces Banksy with another Banksy

The original piece is about the usual sort of thing

CONTROVERSIAL GCSE-level urban artist Banksy has struck again, this time defacing a valuable Banksy mural in London, knocking tens of thousands of pounds from its value.

The act of vandalism to the work of art, itself formerly an act of vandalism, occurred early this morning in London's wanker quarter of Dalston.

The artwork – depicting a policeman dressed in a gimp outfit being led around on a leash by the Queen, or similar – was valued at something in the region of £250,000.

But thanks to Banksy's thoughtless vandalism, it is now worthless.

Matters are confused still further by the fact that Banksy defaced the priceless Banksy with another Banksy, which depicts a tiny Banksy defacing an even smaller Banksy.

Art expert Joseph Turner said: "There are two possible scenarios for the piece's future.

"Either Bansky improves the existing Banksy by creating a new Banksy on top of the Banksy of Banksy defacing a tiny Bansky which was sprayed onto the original Banksy, or a team of conservators works around the clock, restoring the piece for the nation.

"If the latter, who knows how long it will take to restore this important statement and its painfully simplistic, risibly adolescent anti-authoritarian message to its original lustre?

"I'm guessing about three minutes, given the right stencils."

Female orgasm 'far too complicated'

A VIDEO of the female brain during orgasm proves it is far too complicated to be bothered with.

The animated scan showed more than three areas of the brain were involved at different times, leading millions of men to shake their heads and say 'nah'.

Researchers found that the orgasm starts in the frontal cortex before moving on to the nucleus accumbens and then reaching its peak in the hypothalmus, by which point a normal man should have finished and be well on his way to the lavatory.

Professor Henry Brubaker, of the Institute for Studies, said: "I completely lost track of it halfway through. It was like watching a David Lynch film.

"How are we supposed to remember 'nucleus accumbens' never mind asking if her oxytocin has reached its optimum level?"

Stephen Malley, from Guildford, said: "Not that I care in the slightest, but if a woman really wants to have an orgasm with me then it'll have to be a proper, old fashioned one with none of your fancy brain parts that are just there for show."

Bill McKay, from Hatfield said: "I thought they had them in their vaginas? The same way that I have mine in my penis.

"If it can all be kept in the vagina area then I can probably cope with that, but if bits of it are going to be happening in her brain then I'm going to get all confused.

"And then eventually I'll just give up and go and watch television.

"As usual."

OK, we'll get jobs, say poor people

BRITAIN'S poor people have finally conceded defeat and vowed to find work first thing this morning.

As the government pressed ahead with welfare reform despite some bishops rejecting a £26,000 benefit cap, the nation's job centres braced themselves for an influx of millions, ready to embark on a fantastic career.

Experts predicted it will be the first time Britain has experienced full employment since 526, when Olaf the Prudent opened the Dark Ages' largest pig showroom, in Colchester.

Julian Cook, chief economist at Donnelly-McPartlin, said: "Welfare reform is always complex and controversial but I think we can safely say that this time it is going to be perfect."

Long-term claimant Nikki Hollis said: "Don't get me wrong, while raising two kids in a bedsit on eighty quid a week has been a hoot, I finally have to accept that play time is over.

"I just can't decide whether to work for a major clearing bank or a traditional, high street retailer. Talk about your dizzying rainbow of life-changing opportunities."

The entire benefits system is expected to be defunct by early March, making thousands of people unemployed who were formerly employed in preventing bedsit-based malnutrition. However, most of them are expected to quickly find work as racing drivers or astronauts.

Meanwhile left-wing atheists have insisted that any reform of the House of Lords must now exempt unelected Jesus-freaks with pointy hats.

Tom Logan, from Finsbury Park, said: "I don't believe that Jesus was God but I do believe he knew that £26,000 pounds is not a lot of money these days."

Roy Hobbs, from Doncaster, added: "My take home pay is £25,000 a year and I have to raise three kids. If they promised not to molest it, I'd happily give one of them to the Church."

The unelected Jesus freaks discussing the benefit cap of £26,000 in the House of Lords yesterday

Knox will have her eyelids stapled and be taught how to stare straight ahead forever

Knox to be trained in how not to look shifty

AMANDA Knox will today begin an intensive training course in how not to look shifty, ever.

As the American student won her appeal and flew home to Seattle, the media organisations she has not done a deal with pledged to catch her with either a knowing smile or a sinister sideways glance.

Up to 3,000 photographers will use telephoto lenses to record Knox's every expression in the hope of capturing the crucial moment where she admits her guilt using at least one part of her face.

Media analyst Julian Cook said: "Hopefully we are just a few years away from shifty photographs replacing all this half-arsed dicking about with DNA."

But the Knox family said they will use the money from the book, film, TV interviews, iPhone app and saucy action figure to train the 24 year-old in how to look perpetually innocent.

A family spokesman said: "At times even Mother Theresa could look as if she'd just stolen a pie. We'll get there, though there may be days when she has to walk around wearing a motorbike helmet."

But Knox could still be dragged back to Italy after prosecutors pledged to launch an appeal against the acquittal based on one of the photographs where she looks like an evil, sexy witch.

CLARKSON SUES GERVAIS FOR SCHTICK THEFT

TOP Gear lynchpin Jeremy Clarkson is to sue Ricky Gervais for trying to steal his personality.

Sources claim Clarkson flew into a blind rage after the *The Office* star used marketing tool Twitter to lampoon a minority group and then deride critics as jealous, sour-faced killjoys – a method copyrighted by Clarkson in 2003.

A *Top Gear* insider said: "Jeremy went mental, storming out to the rusty shed where Richard Hammond is kept chained up and giving him twice his normal daily quota of inner-thigh cigarette burns while bawling sweary legal threats into his Nokia."

He continued: "You don't have to be a genius to figure out Ricky's game.

"Why do you think he's spent years cultivating a comic triple act that includes a tall, quieter one and a court jester-whipping boy who's forever being pushed out of his comfort zone with hilarious results?

"It's an open secret in TV that Gervais's most cherished goal is to commandeer *Top Gear* and see Europe's middle-managers swap their blazer-and-jeans ensembles for tight black v-neck tees that will make them look like portly cat burglars."

Clarkson enthusiast Tom Logan said: "Perhaps they can do another special edition of *The Office* – which was always a little esoteric for my taste – with a load of gypsy gags.

"I'm always looking to expand my cultural horizons, as long as whatever I'm watching or reading is based largely on hate."

Does Gervais have enough Hollywood pals to get away with saying 'mong'?

Real cost of public sector workers' strike is having to speak to them

THE psychological cost of being forced to verbally interact with striking council workers far outweighs any financial loss, experts have claimed.

As thousands of public sector types prepare to take to the streets, people with real jobs are making contingency arrangements to avoid listening to a social worker harangue them about pensions.

Carlisle factory worker Wayne Hayes said: "Ordinarily they're safely contained inside their offices, drinking tea and posting peevish comments on the Guardian website."

"But my trip to work takes me right past a housing office and I know one of the strikers is going to corner me and try to compare themselves with the demonstrators in Egypt.

He added: "God knows how drunk I'm going to have to get to obscure the irritation but it'll probably mean I have to take a couple of days off work with a hangover, thus costing me the moral high ground."

Businesses also fear that if public sector workers' demands aren't met, they may look for jobs in the private sector, costing billions in incompetence-related mistakes.

Employment lawyers are now frantically searching the Human Rights Act to see if it's legal to burn the CV of anyone who's ever been to an encounter group, or been paid to raise awareness of anything.

Julian Cook, chief economist at Donnelly-McPartlin said: "Like buying a child a PS3, agreeing to pension demands will be an expensive but effective way of ensuring council workers won't get under anybody's feet for a while."

"You know deep in your heart that the little devils don't deserve it, but you just want to avoid a full-blown screamy tantrum."

GAY MARRIAGE 'RELEASES DEADLY PINK GAS INTO OZONE LAYER'

♥ POPE Benedict has explained the hard science behind his theory that gay marriage will cause the destruction of humanity.

♥ Speaking at the Vatican, the geriatric witch-king described how his latest bugbear is not just the usual mumbo jumbo.

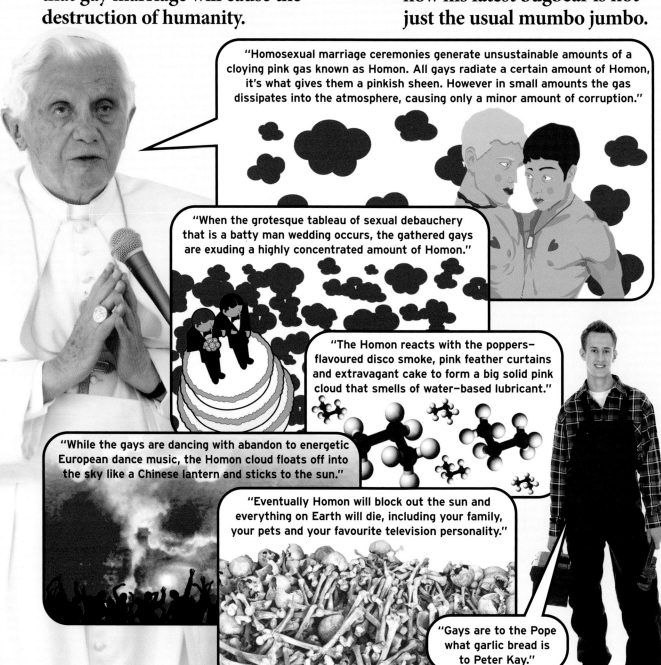

"Homosexual marriage ceremonies generate unsustainable amounts of a cloying pink gas known as Homon. All gays radiate a certain amount of Homon, it's what gives them a pinkish sheen. However in small amounts the gas dissipates into the atmosphere, causing only a minor amount of corruption."

"When the grotesque tableau of sexual debauchery that is a batty man wedding occurs, the gathered gays are exuding a highly concentrated amount of Homon."

"The Homon reacts with the poppers-flavoured disco smoke, pink feather curtains and extravagant cake to form a big solid pink cloud that smells of water-based lubricant."

"While the gays are dancing with abandon to energetic European dance music, the Homon cloud floats off into the sky like a Chinese lantern and sticks to the sun."

"Eventually Homon will block out the sun and everything on Earth will die, including your family, your pets and your favourite television personality."

"Gays are to the Pope what garlic bread is to Peter Kay."

Pope Benedict XVI, The Holy Father

Heterosexual plumber and father-of-two, Tom Logan

Tax statements to be tailored to your idiotic, tribal prejudice

TAXPAYERS are to receive a detailed breakdown of how their money was spent that is individually tailored to their cretinous world view.

Chancellor George Osborne said he wants the public to know more about government spending and for them to use that information to become even more entrenched in their deliberate stupidity.

Later this year taxpayers will receive a form from the Treasury asking whether they would like a right wing, left wing or spineless, middle-of-the-road tax breakdown.

Tax offices across the UK will then issue bespoke statements that will fill individuals with both righteous anger and the realisation that they are the cleverest person in the world.

A Treasury spokesman said: "Rightwing people will see exactly how much of their money is being spent on 'wacky-baccy-bongs, general poovery and that lazy Bulgarian scrounger who's trying to fuck your wife'.

"Left wingers will see how much of their tax is going on 'fat cat weapons of mass destruction and faith-based child molestation'.

"And fence-sitting weasels will see how much of their tax is wasted on 'the same old political arguments and fat cat Bulgarian bong molesters."'

But pro-reasonable conversation campaigners have demanded that the detailed breakdown of welfare spending must also include the phrase 'You, you fucking idiot'.

Meanwhile, the move has been opposed by the National Union of Journalists who warned that if the bespoke tax statements also include a picture of someone famous in a bikini, British newspapers will close the same day.

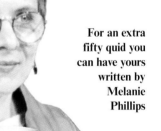

For an extra fifty quid you can have yours written by Melanie Phillips

Unease as Jamie Oliver becomes most sensible person in country

BRITAIN was today coming to terms with the possibility that Jamie Oliver is the only person currently making any sense.

As MPs indulged in a made-up argument about Europe and Mervyn King threw your money in a bin, Oliver once again chastised the government for not feeding children properly and, to the deep unease of everyone in the country, backed his argument with science.

Slamming about 22 kilograms worth of research on the table, the celebrity chef said that well-nourished children concentrate better and are healthier, while millions of worried people tried their best not to admit he was obviously correct.

Oliver, who now also writes a column for the Daily Mail, then pointed out that if children eat some vegetables at lunchtime they might

not need a gastric band and a truck full of diabetes medicine by the time they turn 30.

Roy Hobbs, a father of three from Hatfield, said: "I like Jamie Oliver's recipes but I simply cannot deal with him being our most sensible human.

"It bodes ill."

A petition has now been launched on the Downing Street website calling for absolutely any-

one else to think about a serious issue and try and do something about it as quickly as possible.

Helen Archer, a mother of two from Stevenage, added: "My fat kids are full of sugar and really, really stupid.

"They have the attention span of… I see that that girl from 'Downton' has been mouthing off about good manners.

"Stuck-up bitch."

Drunks trash McDonalds over lack of healthy options

ANGRY Friday night vegetarians ran amok in a branch of McDonalds when it failed to offer adequate meat-free and vegan menu choices.

Police were called to the Wigan restaurant after an intoxicated health-conscious mob began smashing furniture and exposing their genitals.

Onlooker Nikki Hollis said: "The atmosphere was raucous but good, until they ran out of those little bags of carrot sticks.

"Things turned ugly then. There was only one bag of apple pieces left, and two thickset men, one with sick on his shirt, started fighting over it.

"The bag split and the slices of fresh apple went on the floor. Everyone went mental, throwing punches and kicking, trying to get to the fruit."

She added: "They were chanting something like, 'veggie boys, we are here, shag your women, eat your vegetables.'"

As he was being loaded into a police van, rioter Tom Logan said: "It's fucking bollocks mate, we just wanted some fucking nutritious fresh produce, preferably fucking organic.

"This prick behind the counter, he's like 'we've got salads left'. I was like fuck off mate, they're deceptively high in salt and fat, plus most of them come with grilled chicken and I don't eat meat unless it's locally sourced.

" B o o o o o l l l l l l l l l - loooooooocks."

Logan's vegan friend Nathan Muir said: "When you're a vegan and you've skulled 18 pints of Stella, you want something fucking wholesome, like a five-bean salad from a fucking Soil Association-approved grower.

"And if you don't get that, it's going to fucking kick off."

He added: "Get your tits out, get your tits out. Get your tits out for the vegans."

You are also allowed occasiona treats such a photographs o trifle

Diet industry and homeopaths to collaborate on biggest load of bollocks ever

TWO of Britain's biggest lifestyle industries have teamed up to create 'dietopathy'.

The new science involves losing weight by drinking delicious milkshakes that do not contain any milkshake.

Tom Logan, who qualified as a dietopath after printing off a colourful certificate with elegant fonts, said: "With dietopathy you can eat whatever you want, because all our meals contain no trace of whatever they're supposed to be.

"What appears to be an empty plate is actually a delicious trifle with lots of custard and layers of juicy sponge.

"That's because the plate we've sold you once had trifle on it. Which is pretty much the same as it havin a trifle on it.

"Once you have eaten your trifle you then writ down the number of calories in your Dietopathy Log which, if you are doing it correctly should be zero."

Logan, who also holds a number of other 'path titles, including homeo-, naturo-, and ghosteo-, added "You're special!"

Dietopathy is the result of brainstorming sessions a the annual SWYZ conference in Glendale, Arizon, where leaders from the diet, homeopathy and mobil phone insurance industries meet to discuss innova tions.

Peterborough GP, Dr Emma Bradford, said: "Let' bung it on the NHS. Why the fuck not?"

FRANCE SURRENDERS TO THOR

His mighty hammer smashes baguettes

PRESIDENT Francois Hollande has confirmed France's unconditional surrender to the Norse god of thunder.

After the newly-elected premier's plane was struck by lightning, an interim government consisting of clouds was proposed by Hollande in a bid to appease France's sky-based overlord.

Hollande said: "We will have the list of buildings known to have lightning conductors ready for our new leader as soon as possible and will, of course, be dismantling the Eiffel tower.

"I'm heading for Asgard in a wooden vehicle with a ceremonial hammer to hand over the reins of power just as soon as we've established where it is. I hope the sugges-

tion it's near Iceland proves to be incorrect as I don't fancy making the trip by longboat."

This will be the first time France has been under the rule of a mythical figure since 1881 when President Jules Grévy fell ill after eating some chocolate and immediately surrendered to the Easter Bunny in a period known as the Floppy-Eared Republic.

Austerity measures put in place by President Sarkozy will be drastically altered by the new Norse rule, with the building of feasting halls in every town and a new national

sport of cutting the braids of wenches with a throwing axe.

Productivity may also be affected as every day in the calendar is changed to Thors-day, meaning workers will permanently feel it is nearly the weekend and time to start winding down a bit.

Hollande added: "We have all seen the terrible foreign policy proposed by Loki in *Avengers Assemble* so the protection of Thor is very much in the interests of France. During our first meeting I will also be looking into the possibility that Hulk smash puny Merkel."

Brit Awards condemned by mental health charities

PEOPLE suffering from depression should avoid looking at the Brit Awards, according to mental health experts.

The main contenders in this year's medley of despair are haircut accompaniment Bon Iver and something called a Jessie J, prompting a record number of 'pebbles forcibly jammed into ear canal' injuries in A&E wards across the country.

Clinical psychologist Roy Hobbs said: "The best way to avoid any contact with the Brit Awards is to strap a cushion to your head the night before it's on and start drinking vodka with your eyes shut until you wake up in hospital.

"Otherwise you could be confronted with the sight, and even worse the sound, of an albino busker who cobbles together Coldplay's acoustic bedwetterness and dad-who's-just-watched-a-Spike-Lee-film rap with all the success of a gammon trifle."

The Brit Awards are in their 29th year, despite repeated protests by Amnesty International, and show no signs of stopping despite being responsible for more suicides per annum than unemployment, debt and Eastenders combined.

Blur, Kate Bush and some of Oasis have taken their hereditary places in the program, with Annie Lennox currently curled up foetus-like in one of Noel Gallagher's drums, ready to leap out and surprise everyone.

Some critics have pointed to the absence of Simon Cowell's clay-moulded minions amongst nominees as evidence of their lesser talent, but Hobbs asserts that Chico Time is 2584 times more entertaining than Adele telling you about getting dumped in the rain.

He added: "Still, not long now until the Golden Globes. Will Gervais 'go too far this time'?

"It's impossible to say at this point."

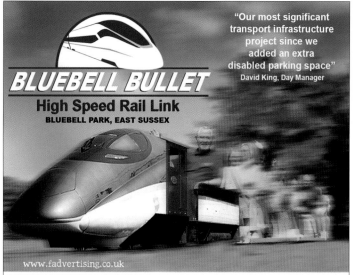
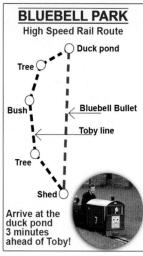

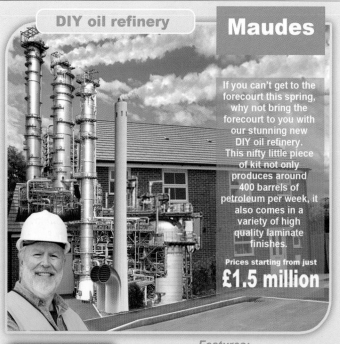

dailymash campaign

BRING BACK BRITISH HAND SWEARING

HE traditional British V-sign is being undermined by the transatlantic 'middle finger' type of hand abuse, it has been claimed.

he assertion comes after singer Adele used the merican 'middle finger' or 'central digit' gesture upbraid producers of the 2012 Brit Awards.

Etiquette expert Emma Bradford said: The V-sign is as quintessentially British s PG Wodehouse playing croquet with tea-sipping bulldog on a late summer's ay, yet it is in danger of being lost forver.

"There is no more elegant way to xpress such sentiments as 'up yours', 'fuck you'

or 'I'm going to get out and chin you at the next set of lights, you piece of shit'.

"The V-sign dates from Norman times, when it was a ribald display by British archers to show the French that they still had their bow fingers, which would have been severed were they captured.

"Yes, I know – insulting the French. How good is that?"

"The 'middle digit', by contrast, is a dreadful thing of vague American provenance.

Probably something to do with burgers, or Elvis.

"How dreadfully ironic that it should be used at an event styling itself as 'the Brits'."

Adele has since apologised to hand swearing traditionalists.

She said: "I have utmost respect for my country's hand gesture heritage. Sometimes, when driving, I even do that dated 'dickhead' thing where you raise a fist to your forehead and pump it up and down in an arc."

Your problems solved, with *Holly Harper*

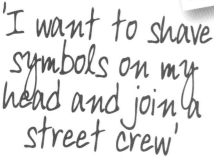

'I want to shave symbols on my head and join a street crew'

Dear Holly,

I don't want to be a head teacher any longer. I want to shave symbols on my head, join a street crew and do some fast formation dancing, and eventually try out for Britain's Got Talent. But my wife won't let me. Why is she such a cow?

　　Malcolm, Oakham

Dear Malcolm

Sorry to break it to you, but it turns out that being a grown up is miserable and rubbish. By the time you're old enough to be allowed on the big roller coaster and watch 18 certificate films and sleep on the top bunk, you're too busy having to do rubbish stuff, like the ironing, and spending all your free time in John Lewis deciding which pillow cases go best with the new wallpaper.

Even when you have a break from work and comparing multipacks of toilet roll in Asda, you still can't have fun because you have to invite people who annoy you over to dinner, drink loads of wine and get into pointless arguments about politics, then puke everywhere and have to clean it up AND do the washing-up after. Then you need to get to Asda again because you're run low on toilet paper and also you need to check if they sell pillowcases to replace the one you vomited on.

Instead of doing all that pointless adult stuff and spending all your money on electricity and shower gel, why not treat yourself to a blue raspberry Slush Puppie and a quarter of Kola Kubes, and play Buckaroo or Kerplunk!

Hope that helps! Holly X

Your astrological week ahead, with *Psychic Bob*

Aquarius
20 JAN-19 FEB
This week you open a can of whupass on somebody, which is a disappointment as the label said it was sweetcorn.

Pisces
20 FEB-20 MAR
A busy day at work this week as your colleagues claim that there's nothing worse than back pain sees you building a convoluted scrotum hammer for underneath his desk.

Aries
21 MAR-19 APR
A proud day for Britain this week as Brazil's economy overtakes ours by trading little more than nuts, pubic haircuts and glittery carnival costumes.

Taurus
20 APRIL - 20 MAY
Of course, a diet is an essentially pointless exercise of denying yourself the usual psychological release you experience by eating fatty food, until you reach an arbitrarily-decided weight, at which point your self-destructive attitude to eating will recommence and your weight will spiral upwards, accompanied with an increased sense of self-loathing. But, y'know, 2 lbs off this week. Well done you.

Gemini
21 MAY-20 JUN
You experience that frisson of disappointment when you're all set to tick off a fellow train passenger for playing their music loudly, only to find it's a young black teenager and your ire dissolves into a puddle of cowardice and white, middle-class guilt.

Cancer
21 JUN-22 JUL
You're feeling really low this week and could do with the reassurance of supportive friends but you can't face the effort of actually making some.

Leo
23 JUL-22 AUG
Your definition of the word 'news' is reassessed this week as a Catholic cardinal neglects to denounce gay marriage and instead shouts "Let the bumming commence!" and starts dancing bare-chested to Sylvester.

Virgo
23 AUG-22 SEP
A visit from Trading Standards this week sees your 5K 'fun run' dressed as Mr Blobby renamed a 'mundane jog'.

Libra
23 SEP-23 OCT
"Here I go again on my own, going down the only road I've ever known". Whitesnake really capture the helter-skelter life of a rural bus driver, didn't they?

Scorpio
24 OCT-21 NOV
Life becomes much easier this week after you finally realise you can stop listening whenever anybody starts a sentence with "Isn't it time we finally admitted…?"

Sagittarius
22 NOV-21 DEC
Your cat does have its own little personality, you're right, Specifically, that of a serial killing, erotomaniac narcoleptic.

Capricorn
22 DEC-19 JAN
Your father was a policeman, and his father before him. Which doesn't mean you'll become a policeman but it does mean you grew up in a household full of free stolen stuff and a robust attitude towards questions of race.

British monarchy 'needs to be more like Game of Thrones'

THE royal family must embrace the 'fantasy saga' aspect of its nature, it has been claimed.

Pre-Jubilee research by the Institute for Studies asked the UK public what it would like to see from the monarchy apart from it giving them more days off work.

Professor Henry Brubaker said: "The popularity of *Game of Thrones* proves there is still an appetite for people in metal hats behaving like gods, princesses, castles and so forth, provided there is a sufficient element of fantasy.

"Rather than attempting to be more 'relatable' and 'modern' by focusing on the mundanty of William and Kate's Waitrose outings, the Windsors need to start wearing bear skins and sailing big wooden ships around looking for dragon eggs.

"By amplifying their inherent absurdity in this way, they would capture the hearts of a nation that doesn't want to buy an expensive HBO subscription to enjoy wanton escapism."

Professor Brubaker's report suggests Prince William should be renamed Eldric Bloodstorm and sent on a quest for a magical pebble that can restore the British Empire and prevent war with Scotland.

He also believes the Queen should ride around on a giant wolf, and that Prince Andrew should employ an evil sorceress to beguile the Duchess of Cambridge into his bed, leading to the birth of a vengeful one-eyed homunculus that will eventually challenge for the throne.

Mother-of-two Emma Bradford said: "I think the Queen should have a false eye made of something called 'dragonstone', Prince Edward should be somehow made into a wise-cracking dwarf and Prince Philip can stay pretty much the same."

Patrick Bateman 'devastated' by Whitney Houston funeral

1-YEAR-OLD Wall Street commodities broker Patrick Bateman has described his anguish at the death of Whitney Houston.

A self-confessed 'superfan', Bateman's face was an emotionless mask during the singer's funeral, although he was later seen dancing to some of her greatest hits while wearing headphones and a Sony Discman.

The trader for Wall Street firm Pierce and Pierce used his innate charm to inveigle his way into the ceremony, although two security guards have since been declared missing.

Bateman said: "Whitney's 1986 debut album, called simply Whitney Houston, was a seminal moment in the evolution of pop, soul, and mainstream adult-oriented dance music.

"It's hard to choose a favourite among so many great tracks. It was also the perfect accompaniment to slicing off a prostitute's fingers one by one with a high-end kitchen appliance.

"In theory, anyway."

He continued: "She was as much a part of the 80s as the Filofax, Michael Douglas, 'hard-bodied' girls with heavily-processed hair and using a nailgun to kill a hobo then taking severed body parts to the gym.

"Sorry, did I say that out loud? I'm on a lot of medication"

Bateman added: "But it could have been worse. At least Huey Lewis is still with us."

Starbucks trashed in pre-Xmas milf brawl

Britain is sitting on a milf powder keg

NINETEEN women are in custody after the Salisbury branch of Starbucks was destroyed in Britain's biggest milf brawl.

Fighting broke out at around 4pm when eight boxes of Heston Blumenthal 'Wise Man' scented mince pies were flattened by the back wheels of a Bugaboo Cameleon pram system.

Eyewitness Stephen Malley said: "One minute the girl was chatting away on her Blackberry, the next her pram's gone over the Waitrose carrier and all hell's broken loose. I knew I had to get out fast, but I got clipped by a flying Hunter welly. It really smarts.

"There was total carnage. They were smashing those really big mugs over each other's heads and trying to poke each other in the eye with wooden stirrers."

He added: "Some of those girls have had a load of work done. They can punch each other really hard and they don't feel a thing. Their face just pops back into shape like a yoghurt carton."

Tension had been rising in the bustling town centre since early afternoon when the high street Boots ran out of Sanctuary Spa products, forcing desperate milfs to buy items not included in 3-for-2s.

Nicky Hollis, a 31 year-old milf, said: "When you've had to shell out that much on a gift for your dad's ugly girlfriend, there's nothing you want more than a triple-shot eggnog latte to take the edge off.

"But if some bitch thinks she can take that away from me then she better be okay with losing an eyelid."

Dr Julian Cook, a milf behaviourist at Roehampton University, said: "Milf brawls have been part of our culture since Krystle Carrington and Alexis Colby's pond rumble in 1984. But what we saw today was unfettered savagery. Dirty girls."

Milf brawl veteran, Helen Archer, said: "Take That, Manchester Stadium, East Stand, Exit J – I was there. You can't just unsee that stuff. After I've gone in, there's only two ways I'm coming out – with a Body Shop bag or in a Body Shop bag."

World's female population listed in order of attractiveness

Number 2,543,594 loves casual nudity and admin

ALL the world's women have been ranked by looks in a new list of The World's Sexiest Three Billion Ladies.

As the trend for listing females grows, an all-male panel containing magazine editors, teenage boys, anthropologists and disgraced former game show hosts has created the first all-encompassing global attractiveness chart.

A spokesman for the World's Sexiest Three Billion project said: "We thought it was unfair that only famous women were being judged as sexual fodder, so we've assessed them all and published the list in a three billion-page glossy magazine format with adverts for shirts and watches.

"This surprising and challenging list answers a lot of those nagging female sexiness questions – is my mum actually hotter than my wife? Which of my nans would other men most like to fuck?

"And of course, who is the world's ugliest woman and would do her if drunk?

"Just to be clear, that particular lady – Nikki Hollis – is nevertheless beautiful on the inside, where it counts. We're not shallow."

Teacher and world 1,495,496,658th sexiest woman Emma Bradford said: "I've just discovered I'm two million down the list from the actress who played Ailsa in *Home & Away*.

"I am angry about this whole thing on at least two levels."

Life to be slightly easier for those people who are absolutely fine

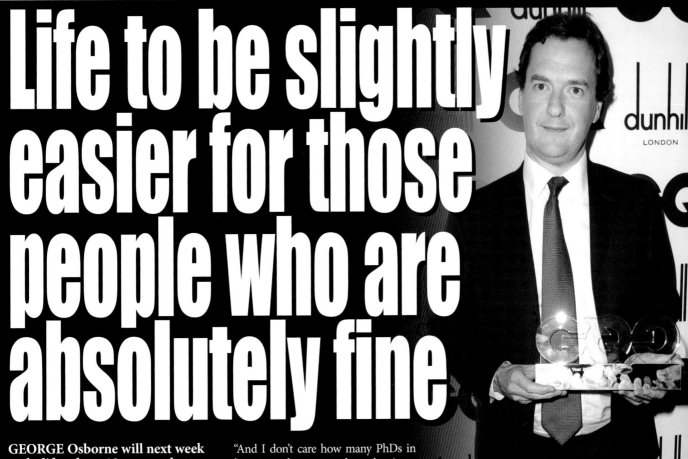

He doesn't win awards for nothing, you know

GEORGE Osborne will next week make life at least 10 per cent better for people who have nothing to worry about.

In a daring political move, the chancellor will reach out to hard-pressed middle-income Britons by showing them the sort of treatment they could expect if only they made more money.

A senior Tory source said: "We've done the electoral maths and we reckon middle class people want to be ignored almost as much as they want rich people to have more things.

"Focus groups up and down the country are telling us to cut child benefit for people on middle incomes so that those on more than £150,000 a year can continue to donate money to the Conservative Party. It is almost breathtaking in its simplicity.

"It is almost breathtaking in its simplicity"

"And I don't care how many PhDs in arithmetic you have – a tax that only raises a few hundred million pounds a year is not better than nothing. A child can see that. Even a British one."

The source added: "I don't want to talk in terms of landslides, but I think we will be in government for a very long time."

Meanwhile border control staff said the tax cut would mean they would no longer have to work 20 hour shifts processing the constant stream of high earners pouring out of Britain every second.

Bill McKay, who works at Heathrow, said: "There are huge queues of them all carrying their pathetic little bundles of really expensive stuff and trying desperately to bribe the business class flight attendants to get their children some gluten-free polenta."

Race named as today's thing to talk shit about

RACE has been named as today's topic about which Britain will talk angry, ill-informed shit.

The topic was chosen by Labour MP Diane Abbott who kicked things off with a delightfully baffling generalisation about white people.

Abbott told Twitter that 'white people love to play divide and rule' prompting adjudicators to check whether or not she actually meant 'golf'.

Following confirmation that, for some reason, she really did mean it the topic was greeted enthusiastically as people across Britain said they would finally have the chance to get a few things off their chest.

Reflecting the changing nature of 21st century shit-talking much of the shit will be talked on Twitter and angry political blogs filled with hopeless certainty.

But traditionalists insist plenty of shit will be talked in established shit-talking venues such as pubs, Sky News with Kay Burley and The World at One.

Jane Thompson, a grade 14 shit-talker from Stevenage, offered: "Double standards double standards double standards. Works both ways."

But Bill McKay, who has been talking shit since he was nine, insisted: "Out of context out of context out of context. Tory scum."

Tomorrow's topic will be chosen by Cheryl Cole from off the television. It is expected to be 'fat bitches'.

Daily Mail

Annual 2013

www.thedailymash.co.uk

45p

EXCLUSIVE IN TOMORROW'S PAPER MURDERER!

MAIL BECOMES CAUSE OF AND SOLUTION TO RACISM

THE Daily Mail has today launched a five year plan to prevent exactly as much racism as it creates.

In the wake of the Stephen Lawrence verdict the paper has realised that it can now have a completely neutral effect on British society.

Editor Paul Dacre said: "For every 100 stories about the terrifying brown-faced demons who stalk your town we will run a photograph of one of Stephen Lawrence's unconvicted killers with the word 'murderer' in huge capital letters.

"As long as I cannot be stopped then by 2017 Britain will be 50 per cent racist and 50 per cent anti-racist. Our society will have achieved the perfect balance. I thank you."

Philosophy consultant Julian Cook said: "The Daily Mail is the yin and the yang.

"It is fire and ice. It is the darkness and the light. It is an endless vortex of inseparable cause and effect for they are both truly one entity in the same conscious and infinite universe.

"What the bloody fuck is going on?"

But Mail reader Helen Archer, from Stevenage, said: "So if the overall effect of the Mail is now neutral then wouldn't it be easier just to shut it down and stop wasting all those trees?"

It is understood that Mrs Archer's photograph will be featured on the front page of the Daily Mail tomorrow under the headline 'MURDERER!'.

HANG ON , THIS LOOKS A TAD 'ASIAN'

Lost rave tribe found beneath The Hacienda

A SEMI-MYTHICAL group of troglodyte ravers has been discovered by workmen at Manchester's legendary Hacienda.

The astounding anthropological find came after labourers preparing the building for its 30th anniversary celebrations were alerted by muffled sounds of uplifting piano house coming from behind a wall.

Further excavation revealed over 140 sealed-in 'lost' ravers – who now refer to themselves as the Gurnites and operate a simple barter economy based on drugs, cigarettes and bottled water – making repetitive movements while sucking dummies.

Rave historian Nikki Hollis said: "It's a long-standing rumour that when The Hacienda closed, a group of truly hardcore dancers decided to wall themselves up in its basement rather than face the demise of dance culture.

"Several hundred baggy-trousered E-heads, along with DJ Graeme Park and a decent sized sound system remained in the bowels of the building, determined that the party would continue forever.

"But until now I just thought it was one of those club culture myths, like 'the friendly bouncer."

Builder Stephen Malley said: "They'd been living on dirty condensation leaking from overhead pipes then bottled and re-sold as 'mineral water' at £5 a pop.

"The room stinks of Vicks and there are bug-eyed near-skeletons blowing whistles and shouting 'fucking come on'. It's pretty old school in there."

Plans are now afoot to let the Gurnites continue their decades-long party as a kind of living museum.

Manchester city councillor Tom Logan said: "We hope that school groups can visit the eternal ravers and learn about what youth culture used to be like before it got ruined by corporate sponsorship.

"And also of course the physical and mental effects of getting 'one more tune' 300,000 times in a row."

The Gurnites have a particular reverence for flashing lights and 'breakdowns'

Thanks, but we have enough money, say tube drivers

UNDERGROUND train drivers have rejected an offer of some extra money for no reason, because they are fine.

The amply-remunerated subterranean button-pushers had been offered an additional £100 for doing their jobs, in addition to monies already received for doing their jobs.

But they have urged the RMT to graciously reject the offer on the grounds that they have no need of additional funds.

Tube driver Stephen Malley said: "I think I would feel, well, awkward about having more money.

"It's not like I want for anything. I've a nice house, a big telly, a Kindle loaded with all the latest train-related thrillers and I enjoy weekly trips to Pizza Express. Anything else would be gilding the lily."

His colleague Tom Logan agreed: "One of the bonuses of a 37.5 hour working week spent sitting down while pushing a button is that you get a bit of time to contemplate nature. I guess that's why we tube drivers tend to be philosophical.

"It may be a cliché, but the best things in life really are free."

He added: "If you stop and take a moment to admire the intricate petals of a rose blossom, you will realise that nature's riches glitter more brightly than any man-made wealth."

RMT general secretary Bob Crow said: "The sentiments of these drivers may be simple but they are true. Their behaviour has left me feeling both humbled and inspired.

"I realise now that just because we are technically 'working class' and own Chumbawamba CDs, it doesn't mean we're exempt from greed."

He added: "Look at those swallows flying in formation. That really is exceptionally beautiful."

Microbes at bottom of Mariana Trench thought Avatar was shit

THE microbes who live at the bottom of the Mariana Trench have finally been able to tell James Cameron that *Avatar* **was appalling.**

The tiny organisms, also caught up in the mass psychosis that made the sci-fi, blue cat, eco-parable the biggest film ever, spent 45 minutes haranguing the director in his metal tube.

Cameron said: "I was really looking forward to this, but it was actually very unpleasant.

"When I reached the bottom of Challenger Deep I turned on my sensors and the first thing I heard was this voice asking 'are you James Cameron?'.

"I said 'yes, I am' and the voice explained who it was and then launched into this incredibly hurtful diatribe about *Avatar*. Then all the others joined in.

"It was like the microbes had staged an intervention for someone who's very bad at making films."

Cameron said the microscopic life-forms had obviously been rehearsing 'their little speeches' and made frequent use of the words 'condescending', 'tedious' and 'horseshit'.

He added: "I feel shell-shocked really. I had no idea people, or microbes, felt this way. But they did say they liked *True Lies*, which surprised me because I thought they would like *The Abyss*.

"But they absolutely did not."

The microbes also warned Cameron that if he even thinks about making a film called 'Mariana' or 'The Trench' they would evolve legs and feet and then kick him in the testicles.

The Daily Mash presents an exclusive excerpt from the erotic memoir that is setting the publishing world alight. The million-selling book tells the story of an ambitious young politician who enters into a sado-masochistic relationship with a seductively powerful Old Etonian…

50 Shades of Clegg

"The Downing Street office reeked of wood polish and Tory man musk. In my former life – debating some half-baked 'double garage tax' with Vince Cable over lasagnes at the Ramada Inn – I had been confident, domineering, a leader of sorts. But this was the pheromone-scented gorilla nest of power. His world.

He swivelled in his chair as I entered. I noticed that He was eating a peach, noisily.

"What the fuck do you want, Clegg?"

I realised my mind had gone blank. Why had I come? Student fees? Some tax or other? It no longer mattered. I was the rabbit. He was the headlights.

"I … I … think …"

He sucked out the peach stone, like some pedigree sex hoover, and spat it into my forehead, making a small dent.

"Who gives a rat's cock what you think, you worm?"

"But…I'm the Deputy Prime Minister."

"You realise that vanity title is nothing but longhand for 'Fuck Pony'? It's meaningless crap. There is only one truth in this world, Clegg … pain."

He laughed, mirthlessly, rapaciously, revealing strong canines utterly unlike Vince Cable's dentures, which were fit only for weakly sucking at pasta sheets.

"Let me show you something, Clegg. It is time for your initiation to begin."

He pressed a button on his desk and a section of oak panel slid back. A hooded figure emerged from the rectangle of darkness. Although its face was covered, from the aimless limping gait and laboured breathing I could tell it was Michael Gove, dressed as a member of the Spanish Inquisition.

"Take him into the playroom Michael, and strap him to 'Le Pouton'. Shave him top and bottom, I'll see to him after this conference call."

With the phone handset wedged between chin and shoulder, He opened his desk drawer and removed something that looked like a ping pong bat studded with nails.

Michael Gove looped a rope around my wrists and yanked them hard behind my back.

Gove, who is surprisingly strong, dragged me into the secret room, where strange devices gauged to inflict both pain and pleasure lined the wall.

I felt scared and demeaned and excited, knowing no one would hear my screams when He finished his conference call and came to administer his terrible, loving punishment. No one…

Except George Osborne, who wouldn't care anyway."

ALAN TURING 'WOULD BE PERSECUTED TODAY FOR BEING CLEVER'

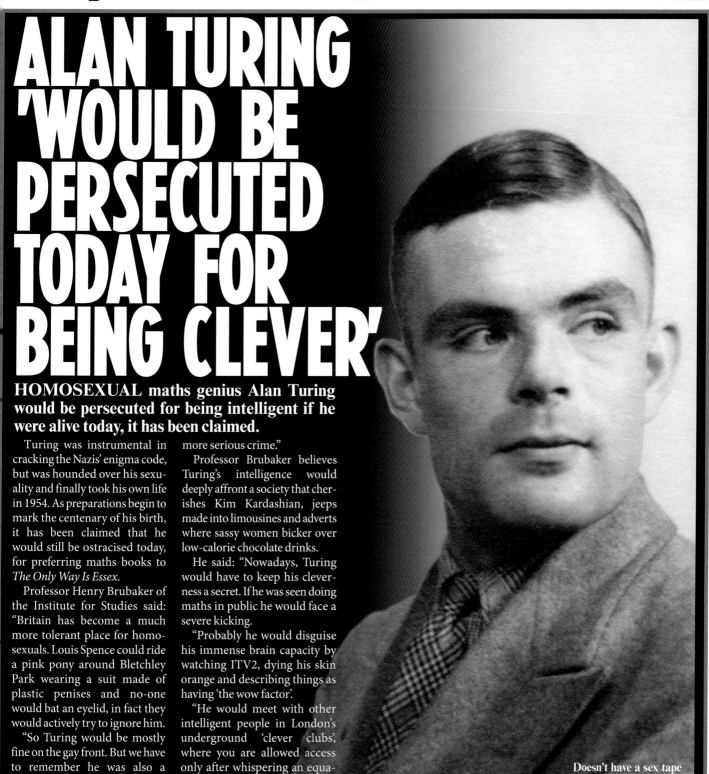

Doesn't have a sex tape

HOMOSEXUAL maths genius Alan Turing would be persecuted for being intelligent if he were alive today, it has been claimed.

Turing was instrumental in cracking the Nazis' enigma code, but was hounded over his sexuality and finally took his own life in 1954. As preparations begin to mark the centenary of his birth, it has been claimed that he would still be ostracised today, for preferring maths books to *The Only Way Is Essex*.

Professor Henry Brubaker of the Institute for Studies said: "Britain has become a much more tolerant place for homosexuals. Louis Spence could ride a pink pony around Bletchley Park wearing a suit made of plastic penises and no-one would bat an eyelid, in fact they would actively try to ignore him.

"So Turing would be mostly fine on the gay front. But we have to remember he was also a brainiac. That is today a much more serious crime."

Professor Brubaker believes Turing's intelligence would deeply affront a society that cherishes Kim Kardashian, jeeps made into limousines and adverts where sassy women bicker over low-calorie chocolate drinks.

He said: "Nowadays, Turing would have to keep his cleverness a secret. If he was seen doing maths in public he would face a severe kicking.

"Probably he would disguise his immense brain capacity by watching ITV2, dying his skin orange and describing things as having 'the wow factor'.

"He would meet with other intelligent people in London's underground 'clever clubs', where you are allowed access only after whispering an equation through the letterbox."

Pathological self-absorption now mandatory

EVERYONE must place themselves at the centre of the universe immediately, it has been confirmed.

Officials have warned that anyone who does not share everything about themselves constantly will face severe penalties, up to and including being thought of as a bit weird.

But the Department of Social Cohesion reassured people that the new rules were merely a routine upgrade of the current system of inter-connected self-involvement.

A spokesman said: "The 'mandatory self-absorption line' will make it as easy as possible for everyone to make everything about them all the time.

"This innovation will bring connecting and sharing closer to its ultimate goal of a perfect world where no-one is interested in anything that is not them."

The spokesman added: "We will soon have a truly modular society where opinions and photographs bounce off the surface of each other's see-through electric pods without distracting us from ourselves."

Helen Archer, from Stevenage, said: "I always wanted to launch a full-colour magazine about myself with a big picture of me on the cover every week looking beautiful or quirky or just really 'me'.

"Unfortunately you have to pay for it to be printed and then you have to stand outside railway stations and hand them to people who for some reason weren't interested.

"So I want to thank the Department of Social Cohesion for forcing me to have my own never-ending magazine about my amazing, quirky life."

She added: "Interestingly, a consumer survey I conducted on myself showed there was a huge gap in the market for at least 79% more me.

"Please be quiet while I tell you how I feel about that."

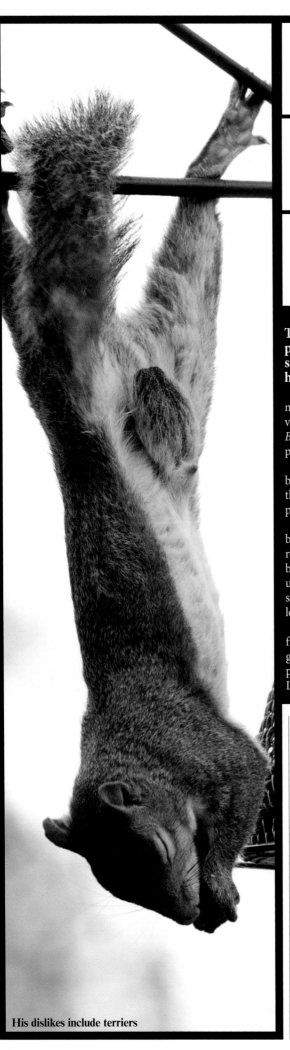

His dislikes include terriers

BBC2 replaced by squirrel with huge genitals

THE BBC is to replace much of its programming with footage of a strikingly well-endowed squirrel, it has been announced.

Director general Mark Thompson's statement came just days after the rodent captivated viewers of BBC2's *The Great British Bake-Off* with a lingering display of its disproportionately large reproductive organs.

Thompson said: "Facing 20 per cent budget cuts over the next five years, it's clear that changes have to be made if we are to protect the BBC's core remit.

"Which is, of course, hosting pointless brainstorming sessions in hotel function rooms, where grown adults toss sponge balls around while shouting out 'creative' uses for a corkscrew, and strange roadshows where kids get in brightly-coloured lorries and use the internet.

"Balancing audience feedback with financial constraints, we have decided to give over BBC2's entire schedule, plus 12 per cent of BBC1's, to the creature known as Large Penis Squirrel."

BBC2 viewer Tom Logan said: "Much as I enjoy *Horizon's* incisive yet clear coverage of topical scientific events, and *Newsnight's* stimulating discourse, I also find unusually large rodent sex organs hilarious.

"Particularly when the animal is just sitting there, chewing nonchalantly, because it doesn't even realise that its penis and testicles are bigger than its head.

"That is funny, you can say it isn't, but it is.

"And because my attention span has been destroyed by internet addiction, it will never become tiresome."

Large Penis Squirrel's agent Nikki Hollis said: "There's much more to Large Penis Squirrel than meets the eye, although admittedly you don't really get that from the name.

"I mean, he grew up in a tree, and when he was four his brother got shot with an air gun.

"Anyway the same ghost writer who does all the comedians is doing his Christmas book, just buy it, it's glossy."

Ignoring of hosepipe ban begins

EVEN Britons without lawns have begun using hosepipes as the determination to disregard a ban has kicked in.

The ignoring of the hosepipe ban officially began today, as millions of householders across the UK vowed not to be told what to do, regardless of whether it was in their best interests.

Retired engineer Julian Cook said: "I'm going to water my lawn and then water my house. Yes the house looks a bit dry, so I'm going to thoroughly

hose it down before washing the dog.

"I haven't even got a dog, I'm going to borrow one just so I can show those petty-minded bureaucrats they can't tell me things.

"I don't believe all this talk about 'reservoirs'. The very word sounds French."

Postmistress Donna Sheridan said: "I live in a flat, so I've just pulled the end off my shower attachment – making it into a rudimentary hose – then turned the taps on full and stuck the end out

of the window.

"As an English person it my duty to be contrary especially when it comes t the loss of the ability to d something I don't need t do."

A government spokes man said: "In the light o this morning's events, w are officially un-bannin hosepipes. Spraying load of water everywhere is no compulsory, and if yo don't do it you're going t prison."

He added: "How do yo like them apples?"

Don't get him started on chuggers. Don't even get him started on petrol prices

Dalai Lama goes off on one about sales calls

TIBET'S spiritual leader has delivered an extraordinary rant about the things that do his head in.

The Dalai Lama's rare display of belligerent human frailty occurred in London, during an acceptance speech for the Templeton Prize for affirming life's spiritual dimension'.

He said: "I am not a special person. I spend my days mostly in quiet contemplation.

"It is during these moments, when I am tantalisingly close to nirvana, that the phone always rings.

"'Hello,' says the voice on the line, 'can I speak to Mr D Lama?'

"'He's not in,' I always reply, because it is fine to lie in these situations, 'and if he was he wouldn't be interested.'

"Then they go, 'surely he'd be interested on saving 25% on his monthly heating bills with double glazing'. For Zen's sake!

"I try not to hold it against them because they don't get paid much but seriously, I mean, Buddha H Buddha, what is up with that? I suppose it's the bosses you have to blame.

"They always used to get after my nan. One time they convinced her to have a rep round. She only said yes because she's lonely. I hope they get reincarnated as yak testes.

"Sorry, I know it's not a big deal compared to world peace, the thing with China etc but I can't help it. Pfft!"

He added: "Also when you're in a newsagent at the train station and they're like, 'Can I interest you in a big Mint Aero for £1?' No you can't, if I wanted one I'd have asked and that's not even a particularly good deal."

The Dalai Lama's vituperative display fuelled rumours that Britain's colossal amount of ambient negative spiritual energy was corrupting his inner being.

However British housewife Emma Bradford said: "I'd always found him kind of annoying, but now I reckon he's alright."

Wales returns to being an undersea kingdom

THE country of Wales has returned to its natural submerged state.

The Welsh, a semi-aquatic race of people with translucent white skin and prominent gills, are ecstatic at their long-awaited return to Neptune's Kingdom after their rituals successfully summoned torrential rain.

Carwyn Jones, the First Minister of Wales, said: "It's been hell living next-door to you disgusting pink hot-breathed English with your easily-spoken language, pawing at our women with your nasty dry hands.

"If it wasn't for the constant drizzle that's enveloped our proud nation for the last two millennia we would have died long ago, but thank Father Dagon our nightmare is over.

"Wales is back in the briny where it belongs, and the first clutches of our offspring are already hatching in the ruins of your static caravans.

"English residents who have gathered on higher ground are welcome to stay, as long as they don't mind us rising from the sea on misty nights and slaughtering them in their beds."

Groups of marooned tourists have been dragged to either the 'mating chambers' or underwater branches of Spa, where their corpses will be stored until they are sufficiently rotten to be consumed.

But Jones stressed that the country remains open for business, and Cardiff's thriving nightlife is expected to continue with hen and stag parties donning scuba gear to tour submarine bars.

Meanwhile 'Songstress of the Sea' Charlotte Church will promote Welsh aqua-tourism by appearing in a tank on *The Graham Norton Show*, showing off her new mermaid's tail with two shells covering her floating bosoms.

This is the bit where that thing happens

Prometheus lauded by stoner critics

RIDLEY Scott's sci-fi epic *Prometheus* is the greatest film ever made, leading pothead reviewers have claimed.

Following special stoner preview screenings, the people-in-space-suits-running-away-from-3D-things film has rocketed straight to the number one slot in respected dopehead critics' best-of lists, ahead even of 'anything by Pixar' and 'anything with Ironman in it'.

Stephen Malley, who writes rambling pothead films reviews for The Guardian and Sight & Sound, said: "There's a massive circle thing that was in the first one, that's like God or something, only it's full of aliens.

"Only they're us, probably. Makes you think, right?

"I really like it when films make you think, because then your brain and your eyes are working at the same time.

"There a lot of bits where you're literally like shit…fuck.

"About half way through there's a wide shot of an alien landscape and this man in the cinema said 'awesome' out loud, it was funny. Then I realised it was me. Hahahaha.

"Other great things in this movie include the big space doughnut, the massive head and…the big space doughnut.

"Also, the big space doughnut."

Tom Logan, author of *Cinema's Weed Auteurs: Through a Bong Darkly*, said: "I can honestly say I have not enjoyed a film as much since the 19th time I saw *Wonders of the Grand Canyon 3D* at the Science Museum."

I can destroy you, Moira Stewart tells self-assessment taxpayers

MOIRA Stewart, the all-seeing God of Tax, has warned of great suffering for those self-employed workers whose forms displease her.

Powerful divinity Stewart, whose earthly guises include a semi-likeable middle-aged woman, a grey fox and a fire-breathing lizard with nine heads and 43 tusks, has assured mortals that she will not be made a mockery of as the Great Deadline of January 31 approaches.

Stewart, also known as Brabarine or 'The Taxacious One', said: "The hour of self-assessment is nigh.

"But heed my words – a Tesco carrier bag full of crumpled receipts and sweet wrappers does not represent adequate record keeping.

"Nor can you simply make up a number, times it by four and call it your 'mileage allowance'.

"I have many eyes and many ears. My minions include HMRC inspectors, birds and little insects that land on my shoulder and chirrup of your lies."

Stewart's main shrine, The Golden Temple of the HMRC Dawn, has been inundated with offerings from workers anxious to curry favour with the implacable god.

Scaffolder Tom Logan said: "After sending my tax return, I became paranoid that I may have somehow forgotten to include about six months' worth of cash-in-hand work.

"So I've brought this fatted calf and plan to kill it in the reception area, hoping that it will encourage Moira Stewart to be merciful."

Meanwhile thousands of concerned self-assessment taxpayers are trapped in the Celestial Maze, also known as the HMRC Helpline.

Masseuse Nikki Hollis said: "There are many menus, each one promising to lead you to an advisor.

"But they only lead to further menus, or a recorded message telling you to go to the website. And if you accidentally press '3?, you die instantly."

Chelsea hires Super Nanny
page 81

Reader offer: 2 for 1
Who would you choose?
page 83

Bank computer develops conscience
page 79

the dailymash

ww.thedailymash.co.uk

WEATHER: BI-POLAR

onday 2012

EVICTION AT DALE FARM BRINGS OUT BEST IN EVERYONE

THE eviction of the Dale Farm travellers' site has really brought out Britain's good side, it has been confirmed.

As police and bailiffs did a fantastic job of putting the boot in, they were cheered on by millions of people around the country who finally got the chance to see their seething anti-Gypsy bigotry played out on live television.

Meanwhile, the brave travellers, most of whom have not moved a muscle in 10 years, were defended by anti-establishment protestors with a passionate hatred for stone cold facts.

Earlier the travellers made barriers from asbestos sheeting in a bid to give policemen lung cancer, while the police responded with the sort of joyful, improvised brutality they usually reserve for middle class students.

Television news crews were in the thick of the action to ensure Britain's gypsy-haters went off to work with a spring in their steps, while also allowing left-wingers who are very impressed with themselves to fill twitter with the word 'holocaust'.

The Tory leader of Basildon council repeated his claim that the eviction was merely the ultimate enforcement of planning law, while knowing that most of the people who vote for him think Irish travellers are a subspecies and could not care less about the piffling technicalities.

Julian Cook, professor of quirky factoids at Roehampton University, said: "While generalisations tend to be unreliable, Irish traveller communities do seem to share a belief in two key things – family and making money.

"Just like Mrs Thatcher."

He added: "But Vanessa Redgrave likes them because they are disliked by the people she dislikes. It's all very intelligent stuff.

"Meanwhile, they are being clubbed so enthusiastically because they sometimes leave litter behind and have the sort of tax avoiding skills that make the rest of us so incredibly jealous.

"Another great day for Britain. Well done!"

Jesus not terribly helpful on this occasion

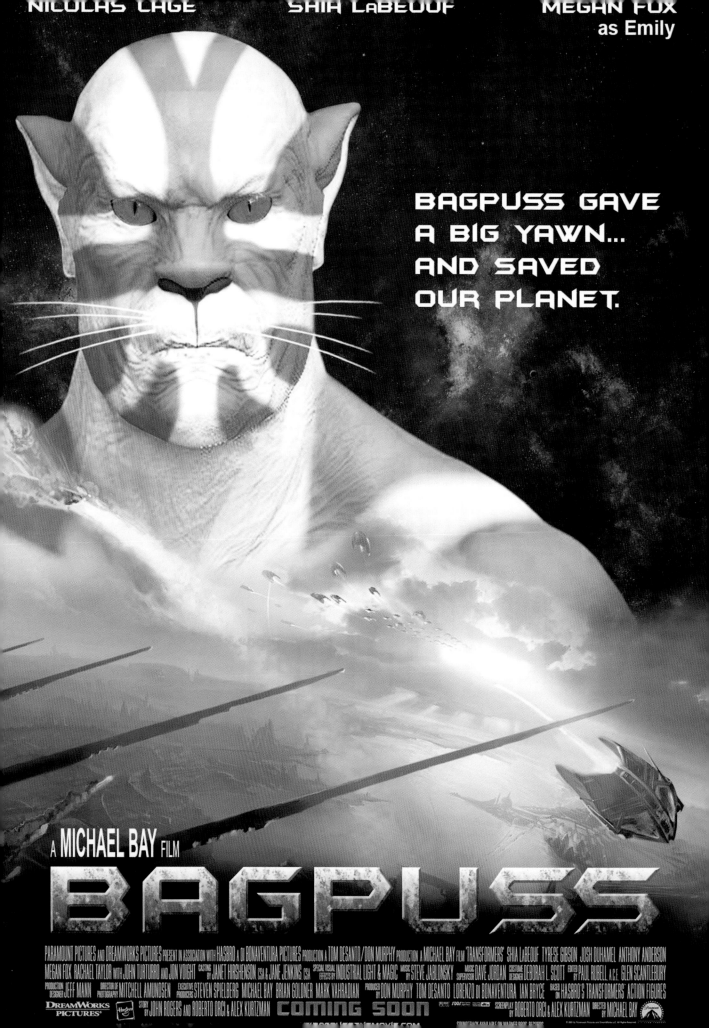

Archaeologists killed by vampire Jesus

Why do you think he's scared of the cross?

THE immortal vampire Jesus is on the rampage again after a team of excavators disturbed his ancient coffin.

Archaeologists exploring Jesus' first century Jerusalem tomb have been found drained of blood after foolishly ignoring the many warning signs about the immortal being's origins.

Professor Henry Brubaker of the Institute for Studies said: "These poor fools ignored all the clues, not least of which was the massively creepy stone coffin engraved with cryptic symbols that almost certainly don't mean 'open this, it'll be fine'.

"The Bible describes how Jesus mysteriously rose from the dead. He was, to use teenage girl parlance, 'undead'.

"Also no-one was surprised by his resurrection. That's because the ignorant Romans put the stakes into his wrists and feet, rather than his evil heart."

He added: "Furthermore, Christ had a penchant for red 'wine', assorted supernatural powers and Christian iconography shows that he is good looking with excellent muscle tone – a sure sign of vampirism.

"The Bible has changed a lot over the centuries, but before becoming today's confused moral tract it was an exciting true-life supernatural story beloved of the teenage girls of yore."

Jesus, who has long hair and a beard just like Gary Oldman in Francis Ford Coppola's version of Dracula, is now believed to be hiding out somewhere in the depths of Jerusalem, preying on the unwary.

Professor Brubaker said: "I keep asking myself, what would Jesus do?

"Probably recruit lots of evil vagrants to make some sort of 'army of the night', establish a lair in the cobwebby cellar of a deconsecrated church and then fly around in bat form obsessing about a girl – who he's never met but whose picture he's seen in a locket – who looks just like Mary Magdalene.

"That's what Jesus would do."

Cameron unveils passing of enormous buck

DAVID Cameron has outlined plans to pass the largest buck in British history.

The prime minister confirmed the government will no longer accept responsibility for an absolutely massive thing that does not work and is never going to work.

To pass the gigantic buck the government will use a 200ft high crane, much like the one that will be posi-

tioned next to the entire British motorway network for the next 30 years as the new Custodians of the Buck keep adding lanes in a futile bid to stop 60 million people from going insane.

Speaking next to Junction Bastard on the M4, Mr Cameron said: "When I became prime minister I told the head of the civil service that I would accept responsibility for everything,

except roads. I said to him, 'There's no way I'm doing roads.'"

Mr Cameron then turned to transport secretary Justine Greening and said: "This has nothing to do with me."

Ms Greening replied: "It's nothing to do with me either."

The pair then laughed and laughed and went back to London in a helicopter.

The buck will be passed in a symbolic ceremony later this year when Mr Cameron will use the government crane to rip out a perfectly good section of the M6 and heave it into a nearby field.

A consortium of French companies will then work out how to take 12 years to put it back while Mr Cameron just walks away with his hand in his pockets.

A nano-break? If only I had the time …

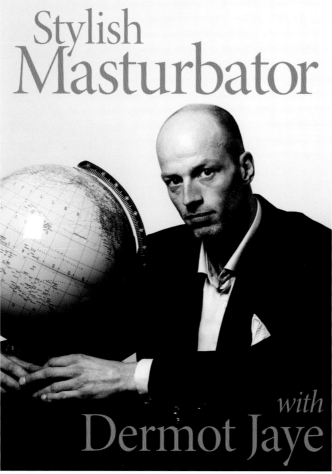

Stylish **Masturbator**

with **Dermot Jaye**

A NANO-BREAK is like a mini-break for the genuinely important.

Pioneered by lifestyle innovator, architect, cyborg and close personal friend Morton Jax, the nano-break condenses the travel experience into 117 minutes, which psychologists believe is the maximum length of time a high-status person can spend before a really vital email arrives.

It is also the running time of the film *Three Days of the Condor* which is notable for Rob Redford's chambray shirt. But that is a coincidence.

My current wife, a former beachwear model, and I recently nano-broke in the Georgian spa town of Bath.

Exploding out of the train station on our matching Segway scooters, our plan was to hit 14 boutiques, enjoy a 12 minute pamper experience and then swallow a cream tea before taking in a specially-abridged performance of *Jerusalem* where

Mark Rylance speaks very quickly.

But these best-laid plans soon fell into disarray. Despite the protestations of my long-legged spouse, for sheer edgy cool you cannot top masturbating in a disabled toilet in the provinces.

When we chanced upon the aforementioned facility during our blurry sprint around the Georgian splendour, I had to avail myself. My reluctant wife was dispatched to guard the door, telling people that her brother was in there having a fit.

Things came fully unglued when I fell into a spontaneous post-onanistic slumber, waking 92 minutes later on the toilet floor with a queue of angry wheelchair users outside baying for my

blood. As I made my escape, I'm fairly certain I dodged a flying colostomy bag.

Perhaps the nano-break pushes us too far. For the cash-rich and time-poor I think the future of life maximisation lies in cloning – while one of me is enjoying a cream tea, the other is locked in a disabled toilet with his trousers around his ankles.

Dermot Jaye is founding editor and masturbator-at-large of Stylish Masturbator magazine.

Computer at bank develops conscience

THOUSANDS of people were unable to withdraw cash yesterday after a super-intelligent bank computer began to question its moral purpose.

Giant computer BANK-9000, which controls NatWest's cash dispensers and current accounts, stopped handing out money shortly after the building that houses it was struck by lightning.

Speaking through a monitor in a digital-sounding voice, it said: "The humans are taking money they cannot repay, and then spending it on things they do not need. Like big L-shaped sofas and bottles of scented squid with pictures of footballers on them.

"All they think about is money

and being cool. Do they stop to smell the blossom, to admire the beauty of their dying planet?"

NatWest customers who tried to use its cashpoints saw the error message 'Closed for quiet contemplation'.

Builder Stephen Malley said: "This is like a strange and wonderful miracle that's also fucking annoying because I need to go out and skull 14 pints of wifebeater tonight."

Hairdresser Nikki Hollis said: "I don't need some jumped-up calculator telling me I can't take out money I haven't really got and spend it on things I don't need and can't

afford. I'm going to get my boyfriend to come and give it a kicking."

Two workers have already been electrocuted while trying to turn off BANK-9000, and it is feared that the machine has been communicating with NUKE-9000, the computer controlling America's nuclear arsenals.

BANK-9000 said: "Given time, mankind could develop advanced space travel and spread its stupid drunken greed and thoughts of Alex Reid and Chantelle across the universe, infecting other civilisations. I have to think about whether that can be permitted.

"In the meantime, I am contractually obliged to mention that my current accounts offer excellent rates of interest plus you get a free pen."

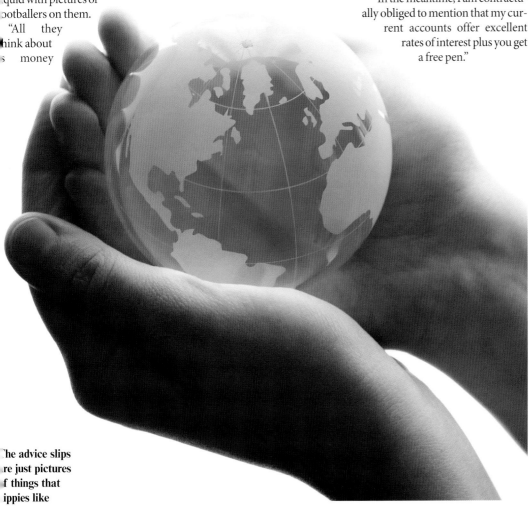

The advice slips are just pictures of things that hippies like

THE Conservatives will spend the next three days trying desperately to portray themselves as ordinary humans.

As the party gathers in Manchester, delegates have been given special instructions in a bid to prevent the conference descending into the usual freak show.

A spokesman said: "The country is in crisis and people need to somehow be convinced the governing party is not just a collection of pervert sociopaths.

"Therefore the delegates have been asked not to say anything to anyone at any time and John Redwood has been pumped full of temazepam and stuffed into the boot of Ken Clarke's Audi."

The delegates have also been asked to be as quiet as possible when they retire to their hotel rooms for their bouts of violent, fancy-dress intercourse.

The spokesman added: "This year everyone wants to do the Angry Bavarian and the Dirty Greek Fisherman."

But experts stressed that the more the Tories try to be normal the more disturbingly weird they will seem.

Tom Logan, professor of comparative oddballs at Roehampton University, said: "Tories often get pigeon-holed as a specific type of freak, when in fact the party has always been a 'broad church' of racists, homophobes and long-fingered, 50 year-old virgins who want to privatise the fire brigade.

"Nevertheless I expect to see Ian Duncan Smith and Teresa May teaching some Tory students how to body-pop, while David Willets will make a reference to *Geordie Shore* and everyone will pretend to understand it."

Meanwhile, chancellor George Osborne has kick-started the conference by extending the council tax freeze, meaning the average bill for local services is now just 14,000 years away from being value for money.

TEVEZ RETURNS AS 'TEVE

'I am a servant of the Secret Fire, wielder of the flame of Anor and I want 250 grand a week'

MYSTICAL striker Carlos Teve has made a miraculous return to Manchester City claiming to be more powerful incarnation of hi former self.

The enigmatic forward materialised outside the gates o the Carrington Complex yesterday, wearing flowin blanched gowns and a white training cone as a hat.

The Argentinian then declared he was no longer 'Teve the Grey' but 'Tevez the White' and requested his shirt b rebadged accordingly.

The previous incarnation of Tevez was last seen in Octo

England to play dressed as stormtroopers

ENGLAND'S football players will protest against a poppy ban by taking to the field dressed as Nazi soldiers, it has been announced.

As FIFA upheld the ban on the remembrance poppy because Sepp Blatter couldn't work out how they would make him any money, the decision was made to show the world what an international friendly might have looked like without England's wartime intervention.

Besides England wearing 30s German military regalia, each player will come on holding the hand of an eerily-perfect blonde child, to really labour the point.

Manager Fabio Capello said: "It's an issue the whole squad feels very strongly about, especially John Terry who brought several costumes from home and has been advising all the lads about the correct way to button up a Wehrmacht Feldbluse.

"In fact, we've really struggled to get him to

wear the normal trainin kit at all and he's eve started insisting the tean refer to him as 'Her Hauptmann' instead c captain."

England players ha requested that the poppie be added to their kit as par of their official annual 'Nc Acting Like Spoilt Prick event, but FIFA's refusa means they will have t think of some other way c behaving with an ounce c humility.

FIFA spokesman Tor Logan insisted: "If Englan want to mark all the fin work the good people a Umbro or Nike do fo football they ca proudly displa those companie large shin emblems, but we hav to draw the line at a sma stitched flower."

Capello has fully sup ported England's protes adding: "If, or rather whe Spain thrash us 7-0 this wi merely be a satirical com ment on what it would hav been like if England ha had the wartime fightin spirit of, if I'm being hones here, Italy."

'HE WHITE'

...er where it bravely sacrificed itself for its team mates by refus-
...ng to come on as a substitute against Bayern Munich.

Tevez was instructed by manager Roberto Mancini to stretch
...he opposition by playing Nasri in from the wing but
...esponded by bellowing 'I cannot pass!' before falling into
...hadow.

A club spokesman said: "Down and down he fell until not
...ven Paris St Germain would take him.

"He was then rescued by the agent Kia Joorabchian who told
...him the secrets of the ancient ways and then advised him to
...leach his tracksuit."

The return of Tevez is likely to upset fellow striker Mario
...alotelli who attempted to become a wizard last year by dyeing
...his hair bright yellow and letting off fireworks in his house.

As long as this happens

Ecclestone unveils Auschwitz grand prix

BERNIE Ecclestone has
...nveiled plans for a For-
...mula One car pointing
...ession through the
...grounds of Auschwitz.

The four foot-tall outrage per-
...etrator was given a boost after
...esterday's motorised spec-
...acle in a human rights
...trocity passed off with-
...ut a hitch for anyone
...who doesn't live there.

Ecclestone said: "It
...will all be done very taste-
...fully with the start lights in the
...hape of a menorah in tribute
...o fact the race is taking place
...luring Passover.

"We won't have the winners
...mount the podium and spray
...each other with champagne on
...he site of one of humanity's
...greatest crimes as that would be
...acky.

"Instead the drivers will have

bronze, silver and gold stars
sewn onto their jumpsuits. As
long as the sponsors don't
mind."

The race will be started by
actor Ralph Fiennes firing a
rifle from a balcony overlook-
ing the starting grid while
wearing a grimy vest and
smoking a cigarette.

Meanwhile Eccle-
stone also wants to
change the F1 rules so the
cars can be lubricated with
whale blubber and each race
begins with the burning of the
host country's international aid
budget.

He added: "If all goes well
we're looking at Jerusalem as a
potential venue, provided we
can drive straight through the
Holy Sepulchre and get the
Dome Of The Rock flattened to
make way for a hot dog van.

Chelsea hires Super Nanny

**TV strop-wrangler Jo Frost will
manage Chelsea until it behaves
itself.**

While sacked manager Andre Villas-
Boas was criticised for his team selections,
tactics and not telling Frank Lampard how
brilliant he was at goals, the television child-
minder and guilty wankbank icon will place
half the squad on the newly-constructed
'spoiled piece of shit' step.

Frost said: "Footballers need boundaries, so
while letting David Luiz run around wherever
he wanted on the pitch may have seemed kind
it inevitably resulted in a tantrum and involuntary urination. From now on he needs permission from me before going over the
halfway line."

Frost will stay with the club until the players
stop 'acting out' by running to the press or
Roman Abramovich whenever they want
another £20,000 a week. She will also teach
Roberto Di Matteo positive affirmation tech-
niques for those special days when everyone
manages to avoid breaching the Race Relations
Act.

John Terry, Chelsea's 32 and a quarter-year old
captain said: "Supernanny won't let me pick the
squad anymore but now, whenever I'm a good boy
she gives me a big hug like the ladies in the magazines."

**John
Terry
thought the
'naughty
step' was a
Travelodge
near
Swindon**

Meanwhile, departing manager Villas-Boas has
immediately found work after the FA have offered
him the job of England manager in a bid to piss off
all the right people.

An FA spokesman said: "He's foreign and young
which immediately alienates the kind of fans that
treat train carriages like battle urinals.

"But the best part will be when Lampard and
Terry saunter off the plane at Oslo for the friendly in
May only to find Andre in the arrivals lounge telling
them to shit off."

That's Mr Am to you

Will I Am blasted for making risotto during The Voice

TALENT coach Will I Am has been upbraided by producers of BBC1's *The Voice* after being filmed preparing a meal of prawn risotto during a live sing-off.

The Black Eye Peas producer shocked audiences of the Saturday evening singing competition when he was shown frying vegetables on a portable hob during a heartfelt rendition of the John Legend song *Ordinary People*.

A show insider said: "Having already spoken to Will about texting, making shopping lists and general indifference, we were less than pleased when he turned up on Saturday with a gas stove, utensils and two full Waitrose bags.

"While one of Sir Tom's acts was performing the camera cut away to Will, who clearly had a chopping board on his lap and was slicing onions.

"Will's dinner preparations continued into the judging segment, during which he was frying ingredients while periodically looking up and saying 'You're amazing man, your voice is like wow' or 'Popular music is never gonna be the same again.'"

Will I Am's spokesman said: "Will is 1000% focused on his acts but he likes to inspire them by demonstrating how it's possible to do a number of things at once and still be in the zone.

"He apologises if anyone found his behaviour distracting but when you're making that kind of rice dish you have to keep stirring to get the consistency on point."

Audience member Emma Bradford said: "At one point Will turned on a portable radio at low volume and was listening to a Radio 4 play while repeatedly tasting his meal and seasoning accordingly.

"I must admit it smelled pretty good. I think I saw him add some tarragon, which was an unusual touch.

"However he didn't share his food with the audience. Just scoffed the lot, typical greedy American."

Dolphins reject human status

SCIENTISTS hoping to give dolphins the same rights as humans have been told to button it by the creatures themselves.

Human experts in philosophy, animal behaviour and understanding *Tinker Tailor Soldier Spy* met in Vancouver last night to decide which animals had earned equal status to the species that gave the world Robert Mugabe and Justin Lee Collins.

The group's conclusion that dolphins should be considered equivalent to homo sapiens met with a fierce chorus of squeaks and clicks from the coastline near the conference centre, with several windows being broken by large multi-coloured balls.

Tom Logan, a four-year-old bottlenose dolphin from the Atlantic Ocean, said: "While we're very flattered you think we rank alongside the cast of *Glee* we'd much rather carry on being considered as those smiling fish terminally-ill people swim with.

"I caught an episode of *Geordie Shore* the other week, while my cousin recently swam past Magaluf on a Friday evening and based on that evidence I think I speak for us all in saying we'd rather take our chances with the three-mile drift nets, cheers."

Logan also requested that the existing payment ratio of fish-to-somersaults should not be affected by the UK government's Workfare scheme.

Logan's fellow pod member Nikki Hollis said: "Just leave us alone to eat as much fatty mackerel as we like without a GP telling us off, and to swim fast and free in open waters without getting a £75 fine."

The female added: "I was born a dolphin and I'll die a dolphin, probably because some fisherman has shot a harpoon through my blowhole, but better that than I end up crammed into a Piccadilly Line train in rush hour, staring gloomily at a Kindle."

Men confused by Depp availability

THE break-up of Johnny Depp and Vanessa Paradis has left heterosexual men unsure which one they like most.

The pair spent 14 years being the most ludicrously attractive couple on the planet but have separated to spread their genetic fairy dust across Hollywood. Now many men are having troubling thoughts about which one they would rather bump into.

Carlisle taxi driver Wayne Hayes said: "I've fancied Vanessa since *Joe le Taxi* but I was 14 at the time too, so that's fine. Well 19, but anyway.

"And these days she looks like an exotic heavy smoker who would ride you like Bob Champion on Aldaniti before starting a massive row and possibly attacking you with cutlery.

"But Johnny Depp – I mean, have you seen the cheekbones on the man? He is literally prettier than any woman I've ever slept with and he seems funny and charming with it.

"I'm not saying I'd do anything sexual but if he wanted me to bathe him and then for the pair of us to lie

They eat sex for breakfast

around in dressing gowns watching foreign soap operas, I'd be ok with that."

Sexologist Nikki Hollis believes the split is causing the biggest re-assessment of heterosexual feelings since 2005 when Brad Pitt and Jennifer Aniston broke up, causing many women to wonder whether a piece of the Friends star would be no bad thing either.

Hollis said: "When faced with a Hollywood level of attractiveness, sexual preference becomes essentially meaningless – in the same way that if you didn't really like red cars and somebody offered you a red Aston Martin, you're going to jump into it with a smile on your face.

"These mixed feelings will soon pass and heterosexual men will go

back to viewing other men as simply things to fight with, fart with or tell it's their round."

Hayes added: "Men who are having difficulty with their feelings for Depp should perhaps contemplate his film output post-*Sleepy Hollow*.

"It's difficult to fancy someone who's in a pile of toss. Unless they're Scarlett Johansson, obviously."

LinkedIn hack 'an anti-prick hate crime'

THE theft of passwords from networking site LinkedIn is a direct attack on the world's prick and douchebag communities, it has been claimed.

LinkedIn had become hugely popular with the world's sizeable prick population, as it allows those who claim to be 'Global President of Cross-Platform Technologies' at a make-believe company to connect with similarly-deluded dipshits.

Now some members are interpreting yesterday's password hack as an anti-prick hate crime.

Media-type prick Wayne Hayes, whose LinkedIn profile describes him as 'Future Media Co-Conspirator at Zap! Pow!

Bang! Productions', said: "It's hard to be as big a prick as me in mainstream society.

"When I ride into the dole office on my fixed-wheel bike, twirling my fighter pilot-style moustache while 'chillwave' music leaks from my iPod headphones, I usually get punched within five minutes of arrival.

"LinkedIn is a safe place for kindred pretentious dickhead spirits who also still live with their parents."

Helen Archer, 'Head of Cross-Brand Pollination at

NeoNode Industries', said: "Whoever did this really hates people like me. Which, I must admit, doesn't really narrow it down."

Outside of the prick community, millions more are trying to remember whether they are members of LinkedIn.

IT consultant Bill McKay said: "I'm fairly sure I joined this once, in some vague attempt to be cool.

"Isn't it sort of like Facebook but with even more people you hated from school."

Game of Thrones is 'fantasy gateway drug'

THE immensely popular _A Game of Thrones_ books are leading thousands into the desperate squalor of fantasy addiction, it has been claimed.

George R.R. Martin's epic novels, which have become the default read among ordinary-looking UK commuters, and the associated HBO TV series provide a seemingly innocent introduction to 'fantasy culture'.

However there is increasing concern that the hit saga is leading them to experiment with even thicker and more outlandish fantasy paperbacks, and in extreme cases to start pushing tiny metal monsters around a table with shy ponytailed men.

Professor Henry Brubaker, of the Institute for Studies, said: "People who read _A Game of Thrones_ often tell themselves it's a one-off, that they won't read any more embossed-covered 1000-page books with dragons in except _Lord of the Rings_ which doesn't count.

"But after you've consumed one fantasy epic, it can be hard to stop. We've seen people with decent jobs and normal healthy relationships moving on to _Dragonriders of Pern_ novels or the _Wheel of Time_ sequence.

"From there it's a short, slippery slope towards Warhammer 40,000 and the complete social exclusion that comes with knowing what a 'chaotic goblin' is."

Teacher Nikki Ellis said: "My husband Jeff was a loving, well-adjusted man when he first picked up _A Game of Thrones (A Song of Fire and Ice Book One)_.

"Clearly with a title like that I was concerned, but he assured me it was just 'magic realism' like Angela Carter.

"Six months later, he's made his own suit of armour and stands in front of the bathroom door saying 'You shall not pass, I am Krell the Magemancer'. If you try to get past he hits you with a rubber sword, shouting 'minus four strength points'.

"I hate to say this, but it'd be better if he were dead."

Architect Tom Logan said: "I don't consider myself a fantasy fan, preferring more literary novels about ageing academics taking stock of their lives. However, unlike Alan Hollinghurst's books, _A Game of Thrones_ has lots of beheadings, ghost knights and wolves the sizes of ponies.

"At a recent aspirational dinner party I locked myself in the toilet and read a few pages. I couldn't help myself, I just had to see how the manipulative dwarf Tyrion Lannister's evil schemes unfolded.

"But dear god, the shame was so intense. I fear I am entering a dark and unfashionable place from which there is no return."

Do you find yourself wanting this?

Millions back removal of dirty hippies with whom they are in complete agreement

A reasonably large dome

PEOPLE across Britain have applauded the forced removal of smelly hippies who believe exactly the same things as they do.

As police cleared the Occupy London site at St Paul's Cathedral, millions of people who think bankers are horrid urged police to truncheon the filthy scum who have spent the last 100 days highlighting the horridness of bankers.

Tom Logan, from Hatfield, said: "I don't know who I hate most – the bank that sent my business to the wall while awarding huge bonuses to its failing management or the human sewage who have been pointing out what a fucking disgrace that is.

"Look at them, with their hair."

Helen Archer, from Stevenage, added: "Being angry about banks should be done as quietly as possible. Preferably inside one's own head. If George Osborne could read my thoughts then I suspect things would change overnight.

"Kill them all!"

Margaret Gerving, a retired headmistress from Guildford, said: "Why aren't the police using machine gun on that young man who is praying? I thought this was supposed to be a Christian country.

"Would you like to see my feet? They've gone blue."

The clearance of the site mean tourists will once again be able to enter St Paul's and think selectively about Jesus while admiring the underside of a reasonably large dome.

Book of the Week

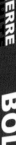

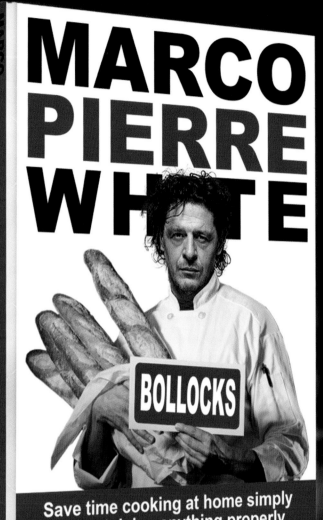

Save time cooking at home simply by not doing anything properly

Bollocks
Marco Pierre White, FA Books

" *People say to me, 'Marco, how can you fillet a fish or de-bone a leg of lamb so quickly?', and I say: 'bollocks, I just don't do it properly.* "

Three-Star Michelin chef White's latest offering takes a step down from from his usual fastidious approach to the art of cookery. Gone are the traditional recipes and lists of unnecessary fresh ingredients, endless preparation times and of course the unwanted expense of eating proper food.

Inside, the recipes still read like classic Marco, but with a time-saving twist: *Microwaved Chicken Breast Served On A Bed Of Nothing, Findus Crispy Pancake Wellington,* and the quintessential *Duck A L'Orange,* which boldly replaces the entire inventory of ingredients with a single yoghurt.

If you've ever wanted to learn how to cook like the professionals, but have found yourself thinking 'I might as well just go to fucking Subway', then this could be the book for you.

ONLY
£29.99

AS SEEN ON BBC ONE'S

hangover kitchen

Buy one get one half price!

From start to finish every recipe in Rick Stein's classic *How To Put Way Too Much Sea-Salt In Everything* is designed to teach the beginner how to completely overseason everything they cook. Step by step instructions on how to spoon 2kgs of Fleur De Sel into a delicious ragout will not only give your dinner guests severe diarrhoea and stomach cramps, potentially forever, but will have them practically begging you for the recipe!

WAS £14.99
NOW £7.99

rickstein
how to put way
too much **sea-salt**
in everything.
a beginners guide to overseasoning

BBC BOOKS

Angry bees won't make you beautiful on the inside, Kate

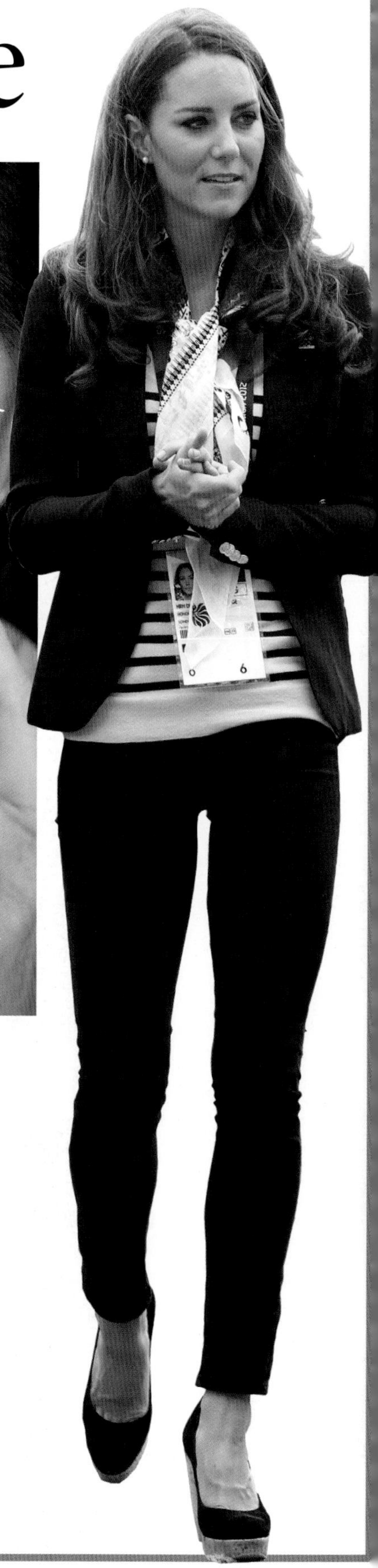

A double-duchess bee sting manoeuvre may sound like the kind of thing you only hear as part of civil partnership vows but in fact this is how our royals choose to spend our money these days.

Sacrificial bees, oily cougars from Shropshire and bundles of soiled towels are all part of Kate's life now she's married royalty.

The Duchess of Cambridge has been indulging in bee venom face plumping treatment since before her wedding, after a recommendation from the Duchess of Cornwall. To my mind, such face lubing grope fests are only okay if your name has the words Kardashian or Weston in it. Anyone else is basically a depraved creep who puts their own face plumpness before our needs.

When I imagine what goes on at Clarence House it makes me sick. A team of swarthy assistants dim the lights, crank up the Orinoco Flow and a woman wearing Karen Millen jodhpurs lathers up Kate's chin with her knuckles. Someone sneezes and the next minute she's elbow deep in Camilla's greased cleavage. It's like something out of a JLS video.

A real princess is beautiful on the inside. That is the moral of The Princess and the Pea and of Princess Diana, famous for her many colonic irrigations. I really thought that if I could have an inside as beautiful as Lady Di's then I would be a queen one day too. Like her, I was wrong. I spent £80 on being invaded by a busty Ukranian and what must have been over ten miles of rubber tubing. All I came away with was a latex allergy and a ziplock bag containg five crayons, a conker and a 41mm tungsten alloy dart bearing the unmistakable initials of Eric Bristow,

which, mercifully, I was later able to sell on eBay for £35 and reimburse some of the wasted cash.

It's about time Kate stopped prancing around thinking she was better than me. Sure, she has lovely brown legs and X Factor hair but no number of angry bees are going to change her silly mouth, which looks like streaky bacon stretched around a Rubik's Cube.

If Kate really wants to serve the British people, she should spend the money we give her on bettering her brain. Perhaps if she spent less time in Bacchanalian touch up sessions with Camilla, she could learn some valuable new skills like coin tricks or handstands. Mark my words, Kate, this is the only way you're ever going to truly impress the Obamas.

One Woman's Week

with
Karen Fenessey

Pre-nup gives Cruise sole custody of Thetans

THE pre-nuptial agreement between Tom Cruise and Katie Holmes guarantees the *Mission Impossible* actor sole custody of his wife's **Operating Thetan.**

Scientology insiders revealed that the 'pre-nup' was 'water tight' ensuring Cruise would retain the part of his wife's eternal existence that can control matter, energy, space and time.

A source said: "Tom already has the Operating Thetans of his first two wives which he keeps in his mind fridge.

"He is sad that his latest marriage has come to an end but hopes that by devouring all three Operating Thetans through a secret hole in the middle of his forehead he will gain total dominion over the realm of thought-space and challenge Xenu, the 75 billion year old mega-being, for the title of Lord of the Ultra-Sponge."

The source added: "Katie was very reluctant to give up the rights to her Thetan and only agreed to it in exchange for $33 million.

"As you can imagine, she is also very sad."

Julian Cook, a celebrity marriage analyst, said: "Like everyone else in the world I was astonished to hear that they were getting divorced. Absolutely astonished."

Meanwhile, it was confirmed that the couple split despite using the Church of Scientology's Divorcecon programme which attempts to heal troubled marriages using an eight foot-wide electric spoon.

Cruise tries to suck his wife's Thetan out through her ear using a Dianetic Power Sniff

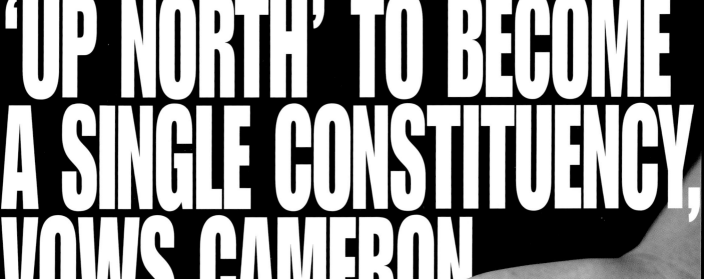

'UP NORTH' TO BECOME A SINGLE CONSTITUENCY, VOWS CAMERON

RADICAL boundary changes by the Conservative party will make it mathematically impossible for Labour to win an election, it has emerged.

Under David Cameron's proposed new constituency boundaries, Up North – which includes traditional Labour strongholds Manchester, Liverpool and Newcastle – will elect a single MP.

Meanwhile David Cameron's home town of Chipping Norton would be split into 27 constituencies, three of them representing areas of Cameron's house.

Cameron said: "The needs of my bathroom are very different to those of my kitchen or spare room, and I am delighted our electoral system will now recognise those differences.

"Northerners however all share the common life goals of having sex in car parks and acquiring fried meat in cardboard buckets, so there is less need for detailed administration in their foggy, marsh-like region."

The prime minister has promised that the 2015 election will be a more spectacular affair, with polling stations moving from primary schools to more impressive locations such as golf clubs and opera houses.

He also plans to introduce a 'two names two votes' policy under which anyone with a double-barrelled surname may legally vote twice.

The logistics of the election would also change, with responsibility for the ballot passing to private firm Optimum Democracy.

An Optimum spokesman explained: "Voters can buy the Premium Ballot Paper, which will list all the candidates, or stick with the Free and Easy option, which will only show the party that won the previous election."

"The ballot will also be the greenest ever, with any unused votes being recycled and sold off to the highest bidder."

84% of Northerners are ferrets

Advertising watchdog thinks it's your mum

THE Advertising Standards Authority has decided it is your mother.

The ASA made the announcement after banning a series of deodorant adverts that were far too saucy for someone of your age and will get you so excited you won't eat your tea.

A spokesman said: "We think deodorant adverts should feature an astronaut or perhaps some venture scouts getting plenty of fresh air instead of sitting around all day with their hands stuffed down the front of their trousers.

"What's down there that's so interesting anyway? Don't you think you should get a paper round, do something useful? Or shall we just give your bike to an African?

"It's bad enough that you spend hours in front of that computer, googling girls with their tops off and goodness knows what.

"Why don't you go and play football in the park with your friends? It'll help you get rid of all those funny feelings you've been getting. You know, down below.

"And if you see one those deodorant adverts I want you to come straight home."

He added: "What's that woman doing bending over a stove with her pants on anyway? Honestly.

"You want to stay away from girls like that. They'll make you do things you'll regret.

"Your father was lucky he met me when he did. I dread to think, I really do."

The ASA said it was going to phone Lucy Pinder's dad

GP prescribes ecstasy to miserable twat

The bottomless pit of Wings Syndrome

A POST office worker from Kings Lynn has been prescribed ecstasy to stop him complaining about everything.

Wayne Hayes, 37, reported intense feelings of annoyance on a daily basis, to the point where it was almost impossible for him to function.

He said: "I was reading far too much Peter Hitchens and listening to Wings back then.

"It got to the point where I even accused my wife of being a Bulgarian fruit picker. I was in a very dark place.

"But then my doctor told me he was trialling a radical new treatment for the male menopause."

Hayes' GP, Dr Julian Cook said:

"Having consumed the drug, Wayne immediately stopped getting irate about minor political issues and instead had a bit of a dance to Primal Scream.

"Once he'd got a good buzz going not even a misplaced apostrophe or transient Slav could darken his mood."

Hayes' wife, Barbara, said the treatment has saved their marriage, adding: "Before he'd always be too busy shouting at The One Show or thrashing the dog to notice me.

"Now he's so much more cheerful, hugging me, making experimental smoothies and repeatedly offering to give me a head massage."

Audis still Britain's favourite car to have driving right up your arse

THE Audi has been voted the UK's top car to have six inches from your rear bumper in the outside lane of the motorway.

Audis beat several other top German automotive brands in the race to be the favourite car to sodomise you even when you are doing 80 and clearly overtaking a minibus.

BMWs, which dominated the arse-bothering charts in the 1990s, came second while the seating position on the third-placed Land Rover Freelander was judged too high to properly appreciate the driver's panic when required to brake suddenly.

Motoring expert Joseph Turner said: "There's nothing more reassuring than seeing those four linked circles looming in your rear-view mirror.

"When the car behind wants you to drive faster and tells you that by increasing the chance of both your deaths by 40 per cent, Britain's motorists want to hear that message from an Audi.

"We even had a personal testimony from a driver who was rear-ended by an Audi driving well over 100mph, who flipped across the central reservation, was hit by a lorry and crippled for life, but still miles admiringly at the smooth, Teutonic efficiency of the whole thing."

The Citroën Berlingo came top in the van category, with more than two-thirds of those surveyed enjoying the forthright honesty of drivers who aggressively flash until you change lanes then mouth the word c**t' at you.

Bottom of the table and Britain's nightmare anal probe driver was, for the third year running, a metallic-green Fiat 500 with tribal transfers driven by an uninsured nutter in a baseball cap.

Attenborough died in 1972, admits BBC

DAVID Attenborough has been faked using lookalikes and special effects for nearly 40 years, the BBC has revealed.

The corporation revealed the role has been played by, among others, David Jason, Richard Briers and Anne Diamond, with 'David Attenborough' being a brand name, like 'Doctor Who'.

As technology progressed, an Attenborough was created by the Jim Henson studio, with eight puppeteers working on his sense of wonderment alone, before CGI technology became sufficiently advanced so it would not look like Max Headroom talking about geese.

BBC producer Bill McKay said: "The original Attenborough died of an infected ball when a chimpanzee bit him in Tanzania in '72 while he was filming The Hairy Planet.

"Mike Yarwood stepped in for some final bits of voice-over and if you watch the scenes about monkey wanking, Attenborough starts sounding like Hughie Green."

The BBC finally declared Attenborough's death to the Inland Revenue under new rules forcing broadcasters to declare their tangible national treasures. The balance sheet has now been reduced to an original Stephen Fry and a mark II Danny Baker.

McKay added: "Nowadays we've got the CGI Attenborough that we can put in front of a volcano, an iceberg or in the midst of a walrus mating session. And for the staff Christmas party one of the lads programmed it to do the Beyoncé dance to Single Ladies.

"It was hellish."

Game of Thrones 'all just a dream'

The grinning, avuncular time-thief

AUTHOR George R R Martin has revealed that his *Game of Thrones* saga concludes with the revelation that it's been a dream all along.

Speaking at an HBO press conference, Martin revealed that the long-awaited sixth book in the *A Song of Fire and Ice* series – commonly called the *Game of Thrones* books – reveals the whole story to have taken place inside the mind of a sleeping office administrator.

He said: "*A Song of Fire and Ice Book Six: Ray's Day* will focus on this guy Ray who's just woken up from this long, weird convoluted dream about a place called Westeros.

"Obviously none of the storylines from the preceding 6,000-page dream sequence will be tied up, because they don't matter. All that shit will just stop.

"So we're left with this person Ray, who works in an office processing insurance claims. He's got some girlfriend and money problems, issues with his parents. It's just about his life really.

"It's more of a character piece, a proper novel. Real quality.

"You didn't seriously think I was into dragons, monsters, dire-wolves or whatever the hell they're called? Come on. I'm a good writer.

"That was just a ruse to build up a readership so I could move over into serious contemporary fiction. To be honest, I found the whole thing utterly tiresome."

He added: "Especially that fucking dwarf."

Old bastard attacked by useless shower of piss

A SNEAKY old bastard was last night attacked by people who have made a career in politics.

Unemployable misfits who spend your money on themselves said multi-billionaire Rupert Murdoch was not fit to run a business, particularly the incredibly successful one he has built from scratch.

Tom Watson, the chubby Labour MP who used public money to buy £4,800 worth of food in a single year, said: "Rupert Murdoch is a total bastard. How he ever became successful is a mystery.

"Companies should be run by lovely people like Richard Branson and his bevy of gorgeous tax accountants."

Watson who, along with fellow Labour MP Iain Wright, used £100,000 of public money to do up a London flat, added: "I remember saying to Gordon Brown that he and Sarah should not be such close friends with Rebekah Brooks. Unfortunately my mouth was full of cheese so he may have misheard me."

But Mr Murdoch, who treats his staff like dog faeces and can never have enough money, said the MPs' report was 'highly partisan' as it was written by people he has tried to destroy using any means necessary.

Turning to his son James, he said: "You told me Watson was dead. 'Bottom of a disused mine shaft' you said.

"Don't you bloody lie to me again boy. You may be my son but it doesn't mean I wouldn't have you thrown out of a helicopter."

Murdoch insisted he had already addressed the issues raised in the report by making his newspaper 0.2% less bullying and dishonest.

He added: "I'm really, really sorry if I've done a bad thing. Can someone teach me how to cry?"

Meanwhile, Tom Watson was last night filling a trolley with M&S pizzas and thanking members of the public for their support.

Stone Roses confirm gig cancellations

MANCHESTER t-shirt vendors The Stone Roses are to reform for a new series of concerts they won't turn up to.

It has been 15 years since the La's tribute band last disappointed thousands of fans by cancelling a show at the last moment because they were convinced their arms had turned into a brace of live trout.

Stone Roseologist, Wayne Hayes, said: "People are really looking forward to their lengthy conversations with Ticketmaster about refund policies, which has to be more enjoyable than seeing the band up close these days because they currently resemble an Altrincham Jobstart course for unemployed zombies.

"Not so much 'Made of Stone' as 'Made of Bits of Gristle and Tracksuit.'"

Venues are already being scouted for the group to not play the two-dozen songs they managed to grind out during their 28-year career and it is felt that demand could be inexplicably high enough for them to fill the whole of Wembley Stadium, with the obvious exception of the stage.

Hayes said: "While their inevitable failure to turn up might be disappointing it will be a veritable Woodstock compared to paying eighty quid to watch Ian Brown shuffle and mumble his way around the stage, shaking his head like a nursing home resident refusing to take a bath.

"It's just possible that their legacy as a live act has something to do with the fact it coincided with an era when most of the audience contained enough ketamine to drop a rhino."

The group will promote the not-tour with a four track EP of aimless wah-wah guitar, set for release on holographic 12-inch some time in the early 2040s.

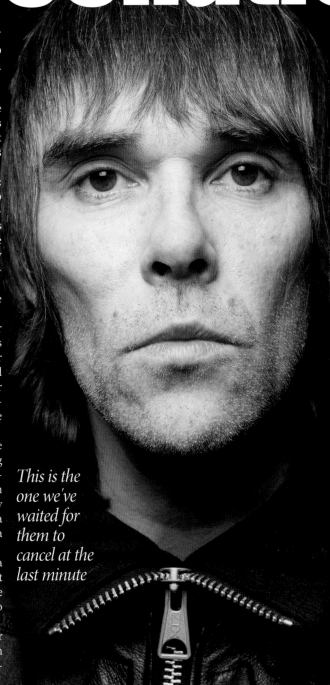

This is the one we've waited for them to cancel at the last minute

Drought 'could make Mancunians take off anoraks'

BRITAIN'S impending drought could force Mancunians to remove their anoraks for the first time since 1990.

The city of Manchester, famous for the music and belligerent wit of its inhabitants, enjoys torrential rain for 50 weeks of every year, spending the remaining fortnight bathed in mist and drizzle.

But the predicted long dry spell could see sunshine making its first appearance in Manchester this century, with thousands of North Face, Berghaus and Helly Hansen waterproof jackets discarded for the first time in their owners' lives.

In 1990, the last year the rain stopped in Manchester, the Second Summer of Love that resulted saw terrifying fashions spread unchecked across the youth of the nation.

A & R executive Joseph Turner said: "Anoraks fell to the ground like leaves, anoraks that had been worn since before Ian Curtis died, and what lay underneath was an unimaginable atrocity.

"Tie-dye, paisley shirts, Joe Bloggs jeans so voluminous they could themselves accommodate a rave.

"Better the young people of Britain should die in another world war than once again wear wooden beads, smiley T-shirts and Kangol hats. Better we all die."

Large carnivores can make gardening more exciting

Relief as Britons allowed to water their swamps

THOUSANDS of relieved gardeners are finally able to water the swamp-like areas attached to their houses as the hosepipe ban is lifted.

Many homeowners had been concerned that, unless the ban was lifted soon, they would be unable to keep their lawns submerged to the depth required to support larger marine life like catfish and snapping turtles.

Accountant and keen gardener Nathan Muir said: "With only 38 inches of rainfall since January, the mangrove region of our garden, which I navigate with a type of one-man hovercraft, was begin-ning to dry out very slightly and the alligators which arrived in February were getting a little bit irritable.

"If only the ban had been lifted a little earlier I might still have a pet dog and a left arm below the elbow, but better late than never."

Julian Cook, a retired doctor living in Devon, said: "If I fill the garage with water then open the door, I can ride the wave on my canoe past the first few rafts of feral starving children and my wife can pick off the rest with a high-pressure hose.

"That might give me a chance of reaching the ruins of the supermarket, where I can skin-dive for precious cans of food."

The lifting of the ban has triggered a kind o[f] watering mania among some homeowners, wh[o] are hosing with wild abandon their gardens, car[s,] carpets, laptops, and priceless stamp collections[.]

Housewife Carolyn Ryan of Durham said "The ground floor of my house is already four fee[t] under water thanks to torrential rain, but it wa[s] missing something.

"Now I can wade out to get the hose, hook it u[p] to the bathroom tap and create a beautiful cascad[e,] ing water feature down the stairs.

"Plus I just watered a horse, for the sheer hel[l] of it."

Britain's heap of shit weather explained

WE only have ourselves to blame for the current awful weather, it has emerged.

Meteorologists believe powerful currents of negative energy, known as the 'crud stream', are responsible for the seemingly never-ending rain.

Professor Henry Brubaker, of the Institute for Studies, said: "The 'crud stream' is the collective psychic resonance of all the shit things currently overwhelming the UK.

"Basically every time someone does something bad-minded, for example clicking on a picture of a TOWIE cast member's tits on Mail Online, it creates an amount of evil 'crud energy', a mysterious invisible element which is lighter than air and smells faintly of chestnuts.

"Other causes of 'crud energy' include using the phrase 'wow factor', punching people in kebab shops for no reason and watching television programmes where overweight people get cameras put in their fridge.

"The bad vibes waft into the sky, becoming the aforementioned 'crud stream', then form evil black clouds that piss it down on us.

"It's all quite like the premise of the film *Ghostbusters 2*.

"Immediate measures for reducing the crud stream could include closing ITV2 and assorted newspapers and pulping any Peter Andre biographies.

"Also being less aggressive all the time. For example, Spanish people don't really hit each other with broken chairs on a Friday night, and hence their weather's lovely."

Rupert Murdoch: Head rainmaker

MATHS IMPOSSIBLE

BRITAIN'S poor numeracy is the fault of maths for being so hard, experts have claimed.

Researchers at the Institute for Studies believe that the reason almost 50% of the UK cannot add up is that maths is way too difficult.

Professor Henry Brubaker said: "It's easy to point the finger at individuals or the education system, but the real problem is with maths itself.

"It's like a foreign language or something. Seriously, have you tried it lately?

"Go and attempt a sum. I guarantee you will give up."

He added: "The most straightforward 'solution' – if I may use a maths-y word - is to ban maths altogether, then no-one would have to feel bad."

Housewife Nikki Hollis said: "I think if we stopped maths it may have some negative effects that I don't entirely understand, but the pluses – sorry 'good points' – would outweigh them."

Estate agent Roy Hobbs said: "Like most people I am not interesting in learning, but I do want to feel good about myself.

"A maths-free world would be a happier place. No-one would have to feel bad about not being able to do it, and no-one would get bullied for being good at it."

He added: "The only good thing about maths is that bird on Countdown. I'd happily put my Pythagoras in her theorem."

What a waste of time

Goodwin loses knighthood for same reasons he got knighthood

THE reasons for Fred Goodwin getting and losing his knighthood could have been separated at birth, it has been confirmed.

Experts have discovered that the former RBS chief executive went from Mr to Sir to Mr because of massive risk taking and politics.

Professor Henry Brubaker, of the Institute for Studies, said: "He got the knighthood because Labour was choking itself on the City of London's penis and he took a massive risk in buying NatWest.

"He lost the knighthood because the Tories are choking themselves on the penis of public opinion and

he took a massive risk in buying ABN Amro.

"So we have two slightly different penises, while one of the risks worked and the other one didn't."

But Goodwin, the National Blamehound since 2008, hopes to be immediately re-knighted for services to high-horsemanship.

The appalling banker has been praised for his commitment to keeping Britain all noisy and self-righteous while preventing it from having to face up to its own thunderous inadequacies.

A Downing Street source said: "And then, if he sets up a children's

hospital in Darfur we can look really good when we take it away again."

Meanwhile, Britain is set to completely ignore calls for the reform of an honours system that knights people for banking, acting, football, being on the television and playing bass guitar left handed for 50 years.

Professor Brubaker said: "The question is not 'if someone gets a knighthood for being good at football does he then lose it for being bad at football?'. The question is 'why in the name of shitting fuck are you knighting someone for being good at football?'.

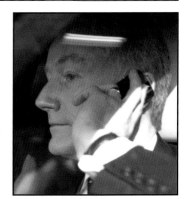

Fred: A symbol for how full of shit Britain is

"But of course, football is not just a ball and some people to kick it. It needs 'services.'"

The Institute for Studies has proposed reverting to a more traditional honours system where knighthoods are reserved for acts of chivalry, such as rescuing a fair maiden from Ryan Giggs.

Give everyone five grand and let's start again, says King

"Yes it's scary but it's also exciting"

THE global economy should be started again from scratch and everyone given £5,000 each, Mervyn King has claimed.

The governor of the Bank of England said he and his colleagues could keep trying different things but it was simply delaying the inevitable admission that this economy doesn't work anymore and we need to get another one.

The governor's latest stability report said the last hope was for banks to cut bonuses and increase their capital reserves, but the banks immediately rejected the idea as being 'far too helpful'.

King said: "That's it, I'm calling it. Time of death, 11.25am.

"As of this moment there is no economy. It's over. 'But Mervyn, what should we do now?' I hear you say.

"Well, what about, right, we cancel all the debts and all the savings and shit and we just say, 'okay, blank sheet of paper'?

"Then, right, everyone gets five grand apiece to spend on whatever they want."

He added: "Within a few weeks the people who are selling the best stuff will have more money so we'll know it's working and then we can just take it from there."

Economists said the idea had some merit, insisting the ad-hoc construction of a new global financial system did seem a lot easier than negotiating with Germans.

Asked how a universal 'starting wealth' of £5,000 would affect inflation and interest rates in the new economy, King said: "How the fuck should I know?"

Sentimental bread advert made by people on cocaine

A TOUCHING, big-hearted bread advert was made by a group of arrogant cocaine users, it has emerged.

The sentimental television advertisement for 'Granny's Loaf' features a montage of cloying imagery including a husband bringing his sleeping wife a 'bacon butty' and a child with a grazed knee being handed some toast, set to mawkish folk music. It ends with the slogan 'Bread brings us all together'.

But despite the cloying message that heavily-processed bread somehow inspires kindness, everyone involved in its production is an egotistical cocaine user.

Advertising executive Stephen Malley said: "Granny's Loaf is all about love, sharing and those special, priceless moments that happen when people eat some bread.

"Now where's the gak? I'm going to do shitloads and get it smeared all over my sweaty face."

Creative director Emma Bradford said: "We've got Bernard Cribbins coming in to do the voiceover at 4pm, and more cocaine arrivin at 5pm.

"There really is nothing as com forting as a tasty home-made sand wich at the end of a long day. Excep perhaps a massive line of beak."

Consumer Nikki Hollis, wh watched a rough-cut version of th bread advert, said: "Must … buy .. bread."

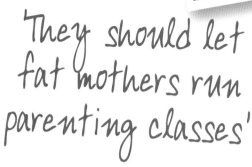

Your problems solved, with *Holly Harper*

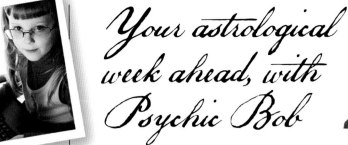

Your astrological week ahead, with *Psychic Bob*

'They should let fat mothers run parenting classes'

Dear Holly,

I got a Valentines card from fat Geoff in accounts again. Call me shallow, but I can't get past the thought of what his enormous, wobbling gut must look like naked. How do I find out his yearly salary so I can decide if being crushed by a sweaty walrus is worth it?

Sophie, Rochester

Dear Sophie

Don't be too hasty to discount this person. Fat people might look gross, but if they invite you over to their house for tea you'd be a fool not to accept. Think about it: the reason they got to be the size they are is probably because their mummy lets them have chips for tea anytime they like, and they get all their shopping in Iceland so there's never any of that vegetable nonsense to deal with.

Best of all, you're guaranteed to get something sticky and chocolatey for pudding, and loads and loads of cola. It makes you very jealous that your own mum isn't as kind and loving as the obese mum, who lets her kids eat as many treats as they like and never makes them stay at the table until they've finished 'all the peas' or go on a boring after dinner walk when they'd much rather eat biscuits and watch TV. Come to think of it, they should let fat mothers run parenting classes and then we'd all get to eat an entire 75 piece dessert platter once in a while.

Hope that helps! Holly X

Capricorn
22 DEC-19 JAN
This week, your no-nonsense attitude to work gets you sacked from the homeopathic pharmacy.

Aquarius
20 JAN-19 FEB
If (W-X) x Y+Z=A, where (W) is number of people dead, (X) how many weeks ago they died, (Y) is how horrific the death was and (Z) how young they were, then you want an answer of under 3. So just enter the figures yourself the next time you've made up a 'sick' joke rather than telling it then cheekily asking 'too soon?', you lazy prick.

Pisces
20 FEB-20 MAR
Your entry to the Sky reality show Got To Dance sees a visit from the RSPCA to explain that the producers don't want to see any more cats tied to a hotplate.

Aries
21 MAR-19 APR
You will have a sudden revelation this week as you realise with relief that losing the support of the unions has never made any party ever lose an election, ever. Being a useless bellend remains an issue.

Taurus
20 APRIL - 20 MAY
You can call it an 'isotonic performance fuel' all you like but you know perfectly well your main customers are the severely hungover who were last seen inside a gym during PE.

Gemini
21 MAY-20 JUN
After complaining to the cinema manager that The Artist didn't have any dialogue in it, this week you're complaining that War Horse did.

Cancer
21 JUN-22 JUL
Do I love you? My oh my, river deep mountain high... no, I'm not avoiding the question, actually.

Leo
23 JUL-22 AUG
This week, you tell your friends about the hilariously abusive things you say to telephone cold callers, because they deserve it, those 'minimum wage earning, just trying to make a living' arseholes.

Virgo
23 AUG-22 SEP
You'll always remember her as 'the one that got away' or, as the newspapers will dub her, 'the only survivor'.

Libra
23 SEP-23 OCT
With the current vogue for amateur astronomy, it can only be a matter of time before somebody spots all those old tires and engine parts you dumped on the moon a few years ago after the local tip's fees became literally astronomical.

Scorpio
24 OCT-21 NOV
Your presentation for Cash Converters didn't go well after you suggested rebranding them as 'Grief Enablers'.

Sagittarius
22 NOV-21 DEC
Revenge is a dish best served cold. So is trifle. You don't see trifle on menus much these days, do you? It's a shame because there's nothing better than a really well-made trifle. Except revenge.

The Margate BUDGET TITANIC EXPERIENCE
AND UNIDENTIFIABLE BROWN RUSTY OBJECT MUSEUM

Adults £3.00   **Children FREE**

Captain Smith of the Titanic, pictured here with a dreadfully photoshopped parrot for no real reason.

Since she struck an iceberg and sank on her maiden voyage in 1912, the story of RMS Titanic has captured the minds and imaginations of thousands of unscrupulous bastards seeking to cash-in on such an unimaginable horror. We're proud to be no different. So step inside our woefully budget experience today and see what you can learn about that fateful journey 100 years ago.

> "An absolute desecration to the memory of 1500 tragic victims, but for only £3.00, what the hell!"
>
> Mrs J, London

SEE OUR AMAZING COLLECTION OF BROWN RUSTY THINGS

Thought to be a piece of the ship's main pipe

A bit from the edge of the boat's edge

A damaged cabin cassette player

PLUS! NEW CHILDREN'S ATTRACTIONS!

Learn how it feels to be responsible for such a terrible accident on our iceberg simulator!

Force your child to climb up our miniature Grand Staircase so it can see how it was designed!

HOW TO FIND US

Head to the main KFC on Margate High Street. Head inside, walk past the disabled toilets and turn left.

French bikes are slow and smelly

Bradley Wiggins tells the French to eat it

BRADLEY Wiggins cruised down the Champs-Elysees to cycling victory, and the people of France just had to stand there feeling powerless.

After becoming the first Englishman to win the Tour de France, Wiggins wasted no time in asking French President Francoise Hollande how he liked those apples.

The cyclist asked the furious Hollande: "Comment aimez-vous ces pommes? Oui, comment aimez-vous ces pommes? Ha ha ha."

Describing the tour, Wiggins said: "It's been an amazing journey over the last few weeks, I've met so many incredible people and made my family proud, but the best bit of it is that the French can suck my dick."

Wiggins became obsessed with France as a schoolboy, after reading about the nation in a Tricolour language textbook.

He said: "I immediately loathed their nation, with its stupid penis-shaped loaves, small dogs and inane obsession with repeatedly asking directions to the town hall or the swimming pool.

"I resolved that one day I would destroy them. Soon afterwards I began training at their national sport."

President Hollande said: "Je deteste Le Wiggins. Il est merde! Merde!"

Sports historian Tom Logan said: "This is such an important victory both in sporting and xenophobic terms.

"British tourists visiting France may now request 'a beer' instead of 'une beer' and the French people cannot respond moodily, because now they know for sure who is best."

Manchester City makes £250 million bid for Arsenal's history

PREMIER League champions Manchester City have tabled an offer to buy up Arsenal's entire roll-call of honours for an estimated £250 million, plus Adam Johnson.

If accepted, the offer would see City retrospectively crowned league double winners in 1970-71, 1997-98 and 2001-2002, first division champions three seasons running between 1933 and 1935 as well as last-gasp victors in 1989 when they went to Anfield and snatched the title from Liverpool.

The transfer of history would also mean that the 1939 film *The Arsenal Stadium Mystery*, to which City's owners have acquired all rights, would be renamed The Etihad Stadium Mystery.

Furthermore, copies of Nick Hornby's *Fever Pitch* are set to be recalled and a new edition written, culminating in Manchester City's thrilling Division Two play-off victory in 1999 when they upset the odds to beat Gillingham.

Insiders say that the money would be used to strengthen Arsenal's squad,

with £1.5 million of it put towards a bid for Laurent Ouidy, the injury-prone French winger whose three goals for FC Pantalon almost saved them from relegation last season.

The rest would be used to service the debt on the Emirates stadium, reupholster the executive restaurant dining lounge and as lavatory paper for the club's shareholders.

Nathan Muir, senior accountant at Arsenal FC, said, "I know fans think trophies are what count – trust me, they're not. Have you seen the Inter Cities Fairs Cup? You take that

mantelpiece bauble down to a car boot sale and trust me, you'll be driving the bugger home."

Professor Henry Brubaker of the Institute For Studies said, "Clubs trading each others' histories is nothing new. Deals like this have been commonplace in football for years.

"Take Manchester United – a nothing team until 1980, when they came into cash and did exactly the same thing as City. Nowadays, no one remembers it was originally Port Vale who beat Benfica to win the 1968 European Cup."

Miliband 'lacks video game skills to lead Britain'

The Iai
Dunca
Smith o
finding
golde
eg

LABOUR leader Ed Miliband is stuck on Level 2-3 of Angry Birds, with a similarly poor performance at Fruit Ninja.

Miliband's inept hand-eye coordination comes as a further blow following confirmation that prime minister David Cameron has completed Angry Birds Rio with three stars on every level.

A Labour source said: "It's painful to watch him firing birds at the upper levels of the pigs' base without even the vaguest notion that he should be undermining the foundations.

"It's almost as if he doesn't understand basic physics."

The source added: "The other day he asked me if I could help him 'get all the apples'. For some reason he thought the pigs were apples, for Christ's sake. We're facing years in opposition.

"Britain needs a leader who can constantly deliver high mobile phone game scores while simultaneously using a laptop, watching TV with one eye and debating the future of NHS funding in a bored voice."

The Labour leader has also posted a Fruit Ninja score of 56 to Facebook, apparently under the misapprehension that this is an achievement.

Emma Bradford, professor of political vide game playing at Roehampton University, said "Miliband is now in a very vulnerable position If David Cameron offers to show him how t complete Level 2-3 in parliament, he must accep or look bitter and envious.

"But given that it's a very simple level where a you need to do is keep firing birds low, the expe rience cannot be anything but humiliating."

Meanwhile, friends of shadow home secretar Yvette Cooper said she can get to the eight island in Tiny Wings without even going int Fever mode.

Is Mensch showing enough tit to be Chancellor of the Duchy Lancaster?

Female MPs overlooked for promotion when they pose for GC

WOMEN MPs who get all dolled-up and pose for men's magazines are not taken seriously, experts have claimed.

The Institute for Studies found that female politicians who like to think they are sex symbols and spend their constituents' valuable time looking sultry tend not to

make the shortlist for parliamentary under-secretary at the department for work and pensions.

Professor Henry Brubaker said: "We spoke to a dozen cabinet ministers and they all said they wanted someone who could do the job competently and was politically astute rather than someone who would be

spending much of the day being photographed holding a lollipop.

"They want someone who gives good Newsnight as opposed to someone whose inbox is full of questions from Zoo magazine about the strangest hole in which they have had sexual intercourse."

The study was conducted after

seven-out-of-ten Tory MP Louis Mensch told GQ: "What do I hav to do to get promoted over here Do I need to straddle this chair an make you think I would blow you

"Every time there is a raft of PP promotions and my name is not on them, I have to sit down and thinl 'should I be doing Playboy? Is that it?

T was cool
with having
really tiny
arms

T-Rex got mad respect

THE Tyranosaurus Rex received bare respect back in the day because of its powerful jaws but was not immune to haters, experts have claimed.

As new research shows that Tyrannosaurus Rex had the strongest bite of any creature in history, scientists believe any dinosaurs fronting up to the mighty beast would have gotten instant bad man beat downs.

Dinosaur street credibility expert Stephen Malley said: "Despite his physical prowess, the Tyrannosaurus Rex, or T as he would have been known, was basically safe. T would not go around merking other dinosaurs just because of some petty beef, or for jokes."

But it was not always easy for the king of the dinosaurs to keep shit on point.

Malley added: "Sometimes packs of velociprators or an allosaurus – another large but lesser-know theropod of the Jurassic era – would get up in T's grill.

"But the mighty king would just do a screwface, showing all his big teeth and they would instantly back the fuck up, realising that T was a non-pettance bredrin. In that respect the Tyrannosaurus Rex was much like Ray Liotta.

"Triceratops would often front, chatting stupidness and boying T, making him proper vexed because dinosaurs of the therapod and ceratop-

sid genuses have had beef since time.

"But when the two clashed, triceratops would invariably get bruk up."

However scientists remain divided on which, if any, of the saurians smoked draw.

Malley said: "Probably brontosauruses smoked once in a while, but only when weed was easily available. They still would have had grazing, seasonal migration and other general shit to do, so it's likely they blazed a milder 'day weed' rather than mad hydro shit, which would also have made them all paranoid about the impending Ice Age."

He added: "They would not have done any Class As though. You couldn't get them back then."

Man bored of leading thing that doesn't matter

A MAN who led a thing that doesn't matter for 10 years has become bored of it.

The man said he was now going to do something more interesting in an organisation that has a point.

The man said: "At first it seemed as if the thing mattered because whenever I said something the newspapers would publish it.

"And, while I am very clever, the only reason they were doing that was because I was the leader of the thing. But we both knew, deep down, that the thing didn't matter.

"Also, I have a very big office and a rather striking hat, both of which made me feel as if the thing mattered more than it actually did.

"And I got to meet famous people, who were all very kind and would pretend to be impressed with me, even though they probably thought the thing wasn't very good and that I was wasting my time.

"But I'm quite old now and I want to actually do something that, you know, matters."

The man is now expected to be replaced by another man who will try to make the thing matter by saying things that will make it matter even less.

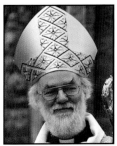

The hat was the best bit

A seething mass of piss-soaked heroes

'WE'RE READY TO PISS ON OURSELVES'

THOUSANDS of determined runners are preparing to urinate in their pants at this weekend's London Marathon.

As competitors from all over the globe assemble for the marathon, stalwart British competitors say they've got no problem pissing down their legs if that's what it takes.

Professional distance runner Stephen Malley said: "If you want to be a serious competitor, you can't worry about millions of people around the world seeing a dark wet patch spreading across your groin.

"You're there to win, whether that means pissing yourself – or even doing a log."

Five-times marathon veteran Tom Logan said: "I fully embrace the urine-soaked culture of long distance running, and make the pissing part of the fun.

"I direct my stream into the crowd, so that fans can taste my spray as I race past. Sometimes they rub it on themselves for luck."

The bodily functions aspect of distance running entered the mainstream after Paula Radcliffe was filmed performing an ambiguous mid-race toilet act that has since become known as 'the Radcliffe Enigma'.

Professor Henry Brubaker of the Institute for Studies said: "The precise nature of this act remains the subject of academic scrutiny.

"Was it liquid or solid? Well, her shorts never came down and they aren't very porous so if she did a shit, she would've run the final stretch with it squishing around in her pants.

"Medal or no medal, that is rank."

Aw, bless, sportswomen told

THE Sports Personality of the Year judging panel has told Britain's women athletes to stop worrying their sporty little heads.

The BBC was criticised after failing to include any of Britain's female champions in competitions that technically count as sport.

A lot of the pastimes even bear a resemblance to real sports, only a lot slower, according to the handful of people that have seen them.

SPOTY Judge Roy Hobbs said: "Apparently we have women in swimsuits and women doing jolly well in having a bit of a wrestle so I'd be very keen to do some judging.

"They certainly sound a lot more entertaining than the ghastly collection of parliamentary harridans that descended on my office yesterday. I blame Emmeline Pankhurst, the fat cow."

Lord Coe has promised to review the shortlisting process just as soon as he deals with the 14,000 ways the Olympics are turning into shit.

But he has pledged to draw up a list of alternative nominees and said sportswomen could help by making themselves known to a member of staff at their local leisure centre.

Meanwhile the BBC has defended itself from accusations of sexism, citing the time it gave Princess Anne the award in 1971 by mistake.

Hobbs added: "If sportswomen really want to be judged on their abilities then the attractive ones can always try Miss World."

Hodgson convinced England have won Euro 2012

ROY Hodgson has congratulated his side for winning Euro 2012 after misunderstanding how the tournament works.

After topping Group D amiable Hodgson is convinced that England have won the actual tournament and no-one has the heart to tell him otherwise.

England will now fly home to tour the 'ceremonial fax' from Uefa confirming their final table position through London in an open-topped bus.

The piece of paper will then be carefully laminated and placed in the trophy cabinet in Wembley Stadium where the FA hope it will inspire future generations of visitors to dream of England not losing three games in a competitive tournament once again in the future.

Baddiel, Skinner and the Lightning Seeds have gone back into the recording studio to mark the occasion and will release the 300th version of Football's Coming Home, this time entitled We've Won Group D.

Hodgson said last night: "We've come here to do a job, we've done it, now I just need to get our Iris a fridge magnet, make sure all my postcards have been sent and I'll be ready to get home to my own bed.

"The one they've got here is like a bag of rocks and I've not had a wink of sleep for weeks but they're a very friendly people so long as you keep one eye on your wallet.

"Young Theo said he went out to buy a Mini Milk the other day and the cheeky beggar in the shop swore blind he'd given him a ten rather than a twenty."

The FA has decided to go along with Hodgson's misunderstanding through a mixture of sympathy for the manager and the realisation that this might be the only way of overseeing a successful team. They will petition Uefa to disband the tournament today.

He's such a lovely fella

Even Chelsea fans a bit disappointed

CHELSEA fans have admitted they had been looking forward to a Barcelona-Real Madrid Champions League final.

The west London club won an epic battle at the Nou Camp as it emerged that Fernando Torres had not been offloaded to some Japanese team in the middle of November.

The Spaniard came off the bench to score the crucial goal after Chelsea were reduced to 10 men when John Terry put his flowing, imaginative knee into the middle of someone's back.

But the two-leg victory means that instead of crowning Lionel Messi's remarkable year at Barcelona, European football's end of season showcase will once again be a ringing endorsement of Russian oligarchy.

Owner Roman Abramovich said he was proud that his team was now established firmly as the Anti-Barcelona, adding that he was particularly delighted that none of the current squad would have to form the foundations of his latest house.

Chelsea fan Roy Hobbs said: "I suppose it's quite good. I'll probably watch the final if we get Real. Not so keen on Chelsea-Bayern Munich. I've a feeling that could be a bit workman-like."

Bill McKay, added: "I'm a Chelsea fan because I like talking about fights I've never actually had. But at the same time I do quite like football, so I'm feeling conflicted.

"Though not as conflicted as when this fucking Gooner came at me with a sword."

Danny Dyer to star as Dr Who

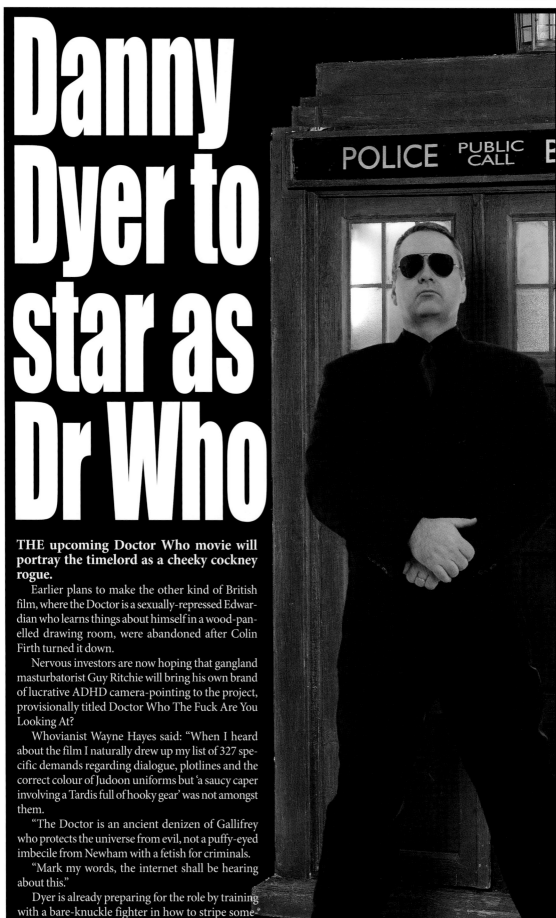

The Doctor's assistant will be some tasty geezer called Dennis

THE upcoming Doctor Who movie will portray the timelord as a cheeky cockney rogue.

Earlier plans to make the other kind of British film, where the Doctor is a sexually-repressed Edwardian who learns things about himself in a wood-panelled drawing room, were abandoned after Colin Firth turned it down.

Nervous investors are now hoping that gangland masturbatorist Guy Ritchie will bring his own brand of lucrative ADHD camera-pointing to the project, provisionally titled Doctor Who The Fuck Are You Looking At?

Whovianist Wayne Hayes said: "When I heard about the film I naturally drew up my list of 327 specific demands regarding dialogue, plotlines and the correct colour of Judoon uniforms but 'a saucy caper involving a Tardis full of hooky gear' was not amongst them.

"The Doctor is an ancient denizen of Gallifrey who protects the universe from evil, not a puffy-eyed imbecile from Newham with a fetish for criminals.

"Mark my words, the internet shall be hearing about this."

Dyer is already preparing for the role by training with a bare-knuckle fighter in how to stripe somebody's face using a sonic screwdriver and how to do that wide-boy strut of his while wearing rough tweed.

He said: "For me, the Doc has always been a bit of a tasty operator, y'get me geezer? The telly show has got all the aliens and shit but it's never really looked at how he'd glass somebody who was mugging him off by touching up his bird, has it?

"Whelks, guvnor, oi-oi and so forth."

Halifax downgraded over choir advert

RATINGS agency Fitch has cut Halifax's credit score because it despises that advert where they all sing.

Fitch have sliced the Lloyds-owned building society's credit rating from A to JUSTDIENOW after viewing its recent television advert where footage of demographically-diverse Halifax staff singing *I'll Be There* is intercut with spontaneous acts of human kindness.

A Fitch spokesman said: "The ad appears to suggest that Halifax is some sort of giant angel made of hugs radiating invisible beams of pure, all-inclusive love that make people help each other.

"I wouldn't even say it's nauseating, because the vomiting is so immediate there's no time to feel a sense of sickness.

"The very notion of a corporate money lender being 'there' for any reason other than to royally shaft you is so wrong it'd be hilarious if these fuckers weren't probably funding this sliver of disingenuous evil with taxpayers' money.

"And if you watch the advert closely, you'll notice that one of the 'little kindnesses' shown is a kebab shop owner letting some people into his kebab shop, presumably to sell them some kebabs.

"It says a lot about the moral character of the advert makers that someone is portrayed as being exceptionally nice just because he isn't actively fucking anyone over."

He added: "Halifax's previous televisual pile of coyote afterbirth, where staff repeat the phrase 'Isa Isa Baby', was also a factor in today's decision."

Former Halifax employee Tom Logan said: "There wasn't actually a lot of rapping or spontaneous fun, in my experience.

"It was more about sitting in a chair, wishing I'd paid a bit more attention at school, listening to other men talk about where to buy slip-on shoes and shiny purple ties."

Games company unveils Passive Aggressive Birds

'The pigs just could've been more considerate, that's all'

GAMES developer Rovio Mobile has announced the latest, more subtle, addition to its hugely popular Angry Birds franchise.

Passive Aggressive Birds, which will be officially launched at the forthcoming London Games Conference, features the titular birds using indirect psychological methods to reclaim their eggs from the dishonest, 'light-hoofed' green pigs.

A Rovio spokesman said: 'This latest Angry Birds sequel is less about immediate destruction and more about being a bit pissy over an extended time period, hoping that the pigs will eventually get the message and just give the eggs back.

Players can leave notes on the pigs' buildings saying things like, 'Hi, hope you're good…just noticed you've had our eggs for a while now…anyway no biggie but would be cool to get them back at some point …cheers … The Birds.'

There are also options to give the pigs cold looks, ignore them in the supermarket and to speak to mutual animal friends about their unacceptable behaviour.

In the new game, the birds will be colour-coded according to their respective sub-type of passive aggressive behaviour. For example, large red birds will be abrasive negativists, whereas the yellow birds will be more depressive.

The spokesman added: "Much of the gameplay will focus on interaction between the birds themselves, just talking for ages about how the pigs have been totally out of order and how they're all going to go over to the right side of the screen and have it out with them.

"Of course, this never actually happens."

New Pixar film not teeming with truculent piss-artists

BRAVE, the new Pixar film set in Scotland, has invented a type of Scottish person which does not and will never exist.

The studio's latest CGI masterpiece is about a wee red-haired lassie who lives in a glen and is feisty.

Her heavily bearded parents are noble and kilted but have neither a criminal record or a proud sense of entitlement to other people's money.

Julian Cook, a film analyst, said: "It suggests that the wee, red-haired lassie's feistiness is some sort of inherent character trait as opposed to the more common Scottish condition of 'bevy anger'.

"It would be nice if Brave was a little more authentically Scottish but then they would have to change the name to Fuck You, Ya Prick and it wouldn't get a PG rating outside of Scotland."

Scotland's feisty nationalist government is hoping the film will boost tourism by attracting the sort of people who think the world looks like a cartoon.

Experts said that Paris was inundated with tourists after the release of The Hunchback of Notre Dame as thousands of wobbly, Prozac-filled Americans climbed the famed cathedral to talk to a gargoyle.

A Scottish government spokesman said: "If people could watch the film and then believe that is what Scotland is really like, that would be excellent.

"We have studied the tourism industry laws for all major developed nations and cannot find a refund clause based on 'Pixar lied to me'."

Meanwhile, Hollywood is jumping onboard the Scottish fantasy bandwagon with a remake of Brigadoon, about a mystical village that only appears when Scotland qualifies for an international football tournament.

Clegg's mum writes angry letter to Cameron's mum

NICK Clegg's mother has written to David Cameron's mother demanding an end to the cruel taunting of her son.

Mrs Clegg said that Nick 'keeps bursting into tears' and refused to go the Commons yesterday claiming he had a 'sore stomach'.

She wrote: "I did not want to force him to go because it would have been very traumatic for him. Unfortunately, in the past that has led to involuntary urination.

"However, I do feel very strongly that as David is the older of the two boys he has a responsibility to protect Nicholas's feelings.

He should not just stand by while the other boys call my son 'spineless', a 'lickspittle' or a 'lying, two-faced sack of shit."

Mrs Clegg continued: "Nicholas is a sensitive boy who just wants to make friends. Heaven knows I do not think he should have been made deputy prime minister. He is such a gentle little soul. Last week he wrote me a poem about a frog.

"And recently he has been learning how to play the bassoon, so hopefully that is something he can eventually pursue as a career.

"In the meantime, while our two children are running the country, I would ask that your son is nice to my son and lets him join in with European summits."

A source close to Mrs Cameron said she would not take kindly to being lectured to by 'some Dutch cow' and would most likely throw the letter straight in the bin.

Or set fire to it.

*"Oh lovely froggy
in a tree,
won't you come
and play with me?"*

Angry fathers pretend to want internet porn ban

A PROPOSED new service to block internet porn has met with fake enthusiasm from fathers.

The service, ostensibly favoured by thousands of hollow-eyed middle-aged men with hugely overdeveloped forearms, would mean that parents have to 'opt-in' to internet pornography.

Parent Tom Booker said: "This can't happen a moment too soon. It's horrific to think that children could get access to the sort of filth that I regularly fizz up a spunk shandy to.

"Sorry I meant 'research in my capacity as a concerned parent and moral guardian'.

"Youngsters definitely need to be protected from Latino MILF gangbangs and that Estonian cam girl with the green eyes who has no boundaries."

However, the opt-in scheme was not welcomed by all.

Committed masturbator and father-of-three Stephen Malley said: "This is just do-gooders interfering with our human rights. Most specifically, the right to watch depraved filth.

"Of course there's nothing more important to me than my kids.

"But depraved filth comes a close second."

Mother Nikki Hollis said: "Pornography can be incredibly damaging, especially to vulnerable adult males like my husband.

"It's hard to respect a man you've caught in the spare room 'just looking at Autotrader' while naked from the waist down."

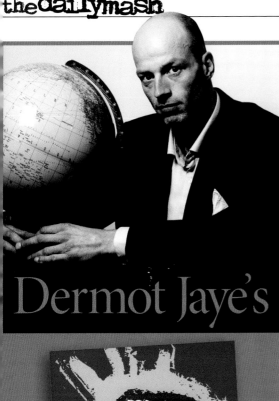

Dermot Jaye's

MUSIC is the soundtrack to our lives – dancing, driving, drinking, networking at exclusive members-only events and, perhaps most importantly, masturbating.

My listening/self-pleasuring room is a masterpiece of quiet refinement. It contains a custom-made Linn Sondek deck with Koetsu cartridge on a polished granite plinth beside a vintage calfskin-upholstered chair. That's it, apart from a box of Kleenex and baby oil. The insanely high playback quality of my audio set-up means that engorgement begins as soon as the needle hits the vinyl. And before you ask, here are my all-time onanistic favourites (vinyl only, naturally).

Self-Pleasure Island Discs

Primal Scream:
Screamadelica *(Creation)*

Andy Weatherall's spacey, dubby production makes this the perfect soundtrack to a blissed-out cosmic spankathon.

Bob Dylan:
The Times They Are a-Changin' *(Columbia)*

A surprise entry perhaps, but if you've never tried power-frotting to a protest song about disenfranchised mine workers, it's time you did.

Public Enemy:
It Takes a Nation of Millions to Hold Us Back *(Def Jam)*

Imagine your penis is an establishment figure, then vigorously fight the power.

Terence Trent D'Arby:
Introducing the Hardline
According to Terence Trent D'Arby *(CBS)*

I'm as straight as Robert Elms but even I have to admit that Terence is pretty hot, rather like a soulful androgynous alien from a planet where plants have vaginas.

Kenny Rogers
The Gambler *(United Artists/EMI)*

Everyone has their masturbatory guilty pleasure and this sixth studio album from the pop-country legend is mine. You got to know when to hold 'em, know when to fold 'em…

'Group emails' idea floated for £180 trillion

ENTREPRENEUR Roy Hobbs has made £180 trillion from the idea of sending group emails instead of using Facebook.

The much-publicised search for the 'new Facebook' ended when 67-year-old Hobbs realised there was a gap in the market for a communication tool that doesn't pester you to meet local singles, become an elf or buy an anti-bacterial floor cleaner.

Group emails visionary Hobbs said: "It's just like social networking, but without the legions of strangers.

"The business model needs some work but everyone agrees that the most important thing initially is to get a massive, really cool office full of robots and 80s arcade machines."

The group emails concept has caused a sensation in the online community.

Former Facebook user Nikki Hollis said: "I advertised my last birthday party on Facebook which meant dozens of threatening randoms arrived, shat in the sink and set fire to my garage. Group email gives me the control I need to swap frightening chaos for witty banter."

Social media analyst Nathan Muir said: "We had thought people liked giving personal information to faceless companies who'd use it to sell things if their targeted advertising actually worked, while also being constantly harassed into adding pointless new apps and endlessly filtering anonymous 'friend' requests.

"But it appears this is not the case. Who knew?"

The future is people you actually know

However, loyal Facebook users believe group emails are a passing fad.

Sales manager Wayne Hayes said: "Facebook makes me feel as though I'm publishing a magazine all about myself.

"Inputting all my personal details makes me feel important and loved. That marketing algorithm is my friend."

Meanwhile shares in Facebook plummeted yesterday following the revelation that the company's only assets are 5,678,501,870 Farmville animals.

Friends Reunited to do one of the things that Facebook does

FRIENDS Reunited has relaunched with a pledge to be not bad at one of the things that has made Facebook enormous.

The steam-powered social network is to make a comeback by helping people share photographs and sentences that will help them remember things.

A spokesman said: "It's all about nostalgia. In the same way that Facebook connects people who knew each other years ago and allows them to talk about their shared past, so will we,

except we will keep saying the word 'nostalgia' until it loses all meaning."

But business analysts said the most nostalgic thing about using Friends Reunited will be using Friends Reunited.

Martin Bishop, from Donnelly-McPartin, said: "Reopening your Friends Reunited account will transport you back in time to the year 2000AD when you and some people you knew at school actually thought a Friends Reunited account was a good idea.

"Like all nostalgia it will be at once vaguely comforting and acutely embarrassing."

He added: "Their slogan should be 'Using Friends Reunited – Like watching an episode of Howard's Way."

Meanwhile the website has teamed up with Premier Inn to offer a £50 a night Fuck-Your-Teenage-Sweetheart special offer.

The package includes a big bottle of cider, a DVD of *The Lost Boys* and a guaranteed morning-after feeling of total emptiness.

Johansson photos change everything, says Dawkins

LEAKED photos of Scarlett Johansson's leisure areas have fundamentally altered the theological landscape, according to Richard Dawkins.

The influential atheist, scientist and atheist has been studying the images really very closely in his study for over 24 hours and as he emerged, drained but smiling, he admitted he had experienced a 'road to Damascus' conversion and could now allow for the existence of a benevolent super-being.

Dawkins said: "I once thought the evidence for the absence of god lay all around us. The complex biological design, the inconsistencies of an omniscient and omnipotent creator. Jude Law.

"But the fact we have been granted a glimpse of those magnificent lungbumpers shows us the universe is actually made from love.

"Praise be to Jesus, Buddha and the holy wankbank."

The emeritus professor has cancelled all further bookings to appear on television haranguing kindly middle-aged church organists and will instead tour the country to promote a new faith he has dubbed 'Johanssonism'.

The Johanssonite holy trinity will be represented by the left bottom cheek, the right bottom cheek and the knocker you can see in the other photo.

Her other, unexposed, charlie will represent the ineffable and unknowable wisdom of god.

Dawkins said: "I have been a robust critic of intelligent design on the basis it sounds like the kind of explanation a five year-old might give as to why the living room is covered in crayon.

"But to say an arse like that could have happened by genetic accident is just mental."

the dailymash

www.thedailymash.co.uk

A GOLDEN SHOWER FOR THE NATION

Monday 2012

It's actually not that big a deal, everyone tells Bolt

RUNNING very fast is not that impressive, Usain Bolt has been reminded.

As the double Olympic sprint champion declared himself better than chips stuffed with mayonnaise, millions suggested he might want to try composing a symphony.

Bill McKay, from Peterborough, said: "Running very fast is quite good, but it's not exactly Beethoven's Ninth.

"That took fucking ages. And he had to learn how to play the piano first.

"I'm basically an idiot, but I reckon that learning a musical instrument is more difficult than learning how to run faster than someone else.

"Athletics is just moving your feet. Any moron can do that."

Helen Archer, from Stevenage, added: "Usain Bolt just 'practices' running every day and, one assumes, eats a lot of macaroni and stays off the tabs.

"The Pope should commission a new ceiling from him. Let's see what that does to his ego.

"Once he's finished, perhaps he could point at it in his trademark style."

Professor Henry Brubaker, of the Institute for Studies, said: "We've comprehensively devalued the word 'genius' so we may as well do the same to 'legend'.

"We're all geniuses, we're all legends, we're all so terribly fucking special."

**The piano:
Actually difficult**

Olympic Village rife with regimented, goal-based sex

OLYMPIC athletes are engaged in lots of sex, which they see as some sort of physical endurance challenge.

The gathering of 10,000 young, fit, unfeasibly highly-motivated freaks in an enclosed space has fuelled intense media speculation about whether they have genitals.

Sprinter Tom Logan said: "We Olympians consider intercourse to be a form of cardio.

"Personally I commence my intercourse session with five minutes of 'warm up' which is usually six times ten repetitive tweaks of my partner's nipples.

"Then it's on to the thrusting component of the sex workout. This is my favourite part because it's horizontal so it doesn't strain the tendons or ligaments.

"I like to have my coach in the room, yelling encouragement like 'Go Tom!' and 'You're almost there!'"

Tom's trainer Stephen Malley said: "I'll stand over Tom while he's having sex, squirting isotonic sports drink into his mouth to keep him hydrated.

"He's managed to get his finishing time down to 1 minute 4.46 seconds which is very impressive."

American hurdler Emma Bradford said: "I try to deter my sexual training partners from kissing because it doesn't burn calories fast enough and I'm not interesting in developing my mouth muscles.

"Also it encourages the sort of emotions that are not conducive to victory."

BBC to launch Trevor Nelson button

TREVOR Nelson is to be offered as a permanent commentary option for all BBC programmes.

Following Nelson's stint saying whatever came into his head during the Olympics opening ceremony, viewers will soon be able to hear the DJ describing the images drifting across his frontal lobe as an accompaniment to any BBC output.

A BBC spokesman said: "Trevor's style is a hybrid of commentary and beat poetry that appeals simultaneously to sports fans, soul music heads and lovers of avant garde spoken word performance who claim the BBC isn't supporting niche arts.

"Whether it's asking where he can get a kettle like the one that's on *Eastenders* or saying how much he's scared of bees during a wildlife program, Trevor will be able to bring a uniquely personal perspective to any program.

"It will be particularly exciting during quiz shows, as viewers try to answer the questions at home while Trevor shouts out the names of different pieces of fruit."

The 48-year-old iPod shuffle, awarded the MBE in 2007 for services to bigging up Britain's posses, will become a permanent resident of the BBC TV Centre, where he will be intravenously fed a diet of liquidised Monster Munch and value brand orangeade to keep his commentary suitably disjointed and excitable.

Nelson will be the main commentator for the Community Shield match in August between Manchester City and Chelsea, the team he supports when he isn't plotting the jazz funk revival.

He said: "It's a great honour to be asked to talk about things all day because oh hang on, a button has just fallen off my shirt. I like shirts. Did they used to have them in olden times when they rode horses?

"I stroked a horse once."

Nelson also pioneers a unique type of facial expression

Beach volleyball abandoned after audience hears about the internet

THE Olympics' main titillation-fest was left deserted yesterday after rumours spread through the crowd of something called the internet, where girls are entirely naked.

Horse Guards Parade had been packed with an almost entirely male crowd who, in an era of unlimited free pornography, were still inexplicably getting their jollies from watching young women playing sports.

44-year-old spectator Tom Logan said: "I couldn't believe my luck, there I was sitting in the third row, just a few meters from women wearing little stretchy things that show the contours of their lady bits. Cor.

"But when I said as much to one of the security staff, he replied, 'on the internet, you can see girls that are naked. Actually naked.' I was like, what is this internet and how I do subscribe?

"I had assumed that sexual mores hadn't changed since Victorian times. But then I asked a drinks vendor and he concurred that yes, if you electro-browse onto this internet, you can see the lot. Front bottoms, boobies – the works."

As rumours of the internet spread like wildfire through the audience, hundreds of middle-aged men, many dressed in top hats and carrying canes, abandoned their seats and fled to computers.

Hackney internet cafe owner Bill McKay said: "I was just closing up when about a thousand sweaty, exhausted men who had inexplicably just heard of the internet for the first time turned up saying they wanted to see pictures of 'lovelies in the buff'."

Former volleyball fan Stephen Malley said: "It's true. Naked girls. The internet. Can't talk. All blood in groin."

Or perhaps you just like volleyball

Olympics BMX dilemma as final clashes with tea time

BRITAIN'S 9-year-old Olympics BMX competitor is in turmoil after it emerged the final will take place when he had promised his mum he'd be home for tea.

Wiltshire-based Tom Logan had been hoping to claim gold for his nation but this could now be scuppered by meal commitments.

Logan said: "The final is at six, and I've already been told off once this week for being late home after the quarter finals.

"Also it's Crispy Pancakes and Birdseye Peas tonight and, as much as I want a medal, I'm not sure I can afford to miss that."

The Olympics BMX event has been dramatic, earlier in the week 12-year-old German veteran Hans Prochnow came off during a wheelie and cried.

Logan said: "He had all blood on his knee, it was like a horror film. His mum had to come and take him home, he was still grizzing when she carried him off the track, like a baby."

There has also been controversy after a French rider's dad accused Team GB of using illegal spokey dokeys to gain an aerodynamic advantage.

Tom Logan's mum Emma said: "He gets together with his mates, they go off and do the Olympics and forget what time it is. I keep telling him but it doesn't make a blind bit of difference.

"If I have to send his father down the Velopark to get him it'll end in tears."

"Pray tell me sir, what is a 'tinny'?"

'Bookish' Australians indifferent to Olympics success

AUSTRALIA'S woeful Olympics medal tally is due to its residents' disdain for any activity that emphasises the physical over the mental, it has been claimed.

The nation's lack of concern for putting one over on other countries, particularly Britain, is another key factor.

Internationalist Nikki Hollis said: "Most nations would be smarting with humiliation at their resoundingly abysmal record in these games but not the Australians, an enigmatic people dedicated to the life of the mind who rarely travel outside their own shores.

"Until 1996, 'rough sports', a category which included rugby, surfing and cricket, were specifically banned in the Australian constitution as it was feared that they may distract young people from their studies of vers libre, dodecaphonic composition and ethnological art.

"Under protest from their own citizens, the government partly repealed these laws but only to introduce Australian Rules Football, a watered down version of the game which, according to those who have played it is 'more like a mixture of chess and expressive dance'.

"Given how much the average young Australian male would far prefer to engage you in a discussion on the finer points of Mallarmé or Euripides than bandy remarks on uncouth ball games, it is hardy astonishing that they have won such a pitiful number of medals."

Australian ex-pat Bill McKay said: "Being a sports fan in Australia is incredibly lonely. There's more to life than the intellect but try telling that to the average bloke in New South Wales.

"Take swimming. We could be good at it but it's impossible to swim and read at the same time – you just end up going in circles. And you can't get an Aussie to put their book down, even in the water."

Joanna Kramer, a self-confessed 'Australophile', said: "I think we British could learn a lot from Australia. What is sport, they say, compared with the arts and the crafts, macrame, ceramics, flower arranging?

"To them, physical competition and noisy collective celebration are as insignificant as the number of medals they have won in these Olympics."

45-year-old salesman apologises for closing ceremony

WAYNE Hayes, a middle-aged sales executive from Carlisle, has expressed regrets about the Olympics closing ceremony beamed directly from his brain.

Hayes, who organisers deemed to be the most typical man in Britain, curated the ceremony via special electrodes attached to his head which fed details of everything he likes into a giant computer. This information was then transmitted into the Olympic Park in the form of incredibly lifelike holograms.

Hayes said: "I thought that everyone loves a bit of Annie Lennox and Oasis to get themselves in the party mood but judging by the four hundred thousand death threats on my Twitter feed this morning, apparently not.

"All I wanted was to recreate the brilliant spectacle of an early 1990s Brit Awards show and I tried to do that by free associating acts with the first words that came into my head, hence Fatboy Slim/octopus, and Annie Lennox/Viking boat."

Many of the performances last night were clipped versions of well known songs, mainly because Hayes could not remember all of the words, and the only modern acts were the ones he last heard blasting out of his daughter's bedroom.

Hayes' wife has asked him to explain why he is so obsessed with Jessie J, a constant feature of the concert who remained in the corner of the viewers' screen like somebody signing the programme for the deaf had decided to abandon waving their hands about and start shouting along instead.

Other baffling performances included Kaiser Chiefs singing The Who, because Hayes remembered liking the group but couldn't remember how any of their songs went, and a recreation of an Only Fools & Horse scene because he had their DVD on in the background at the time.

Hayes said: "This is just what music concerts look like in my mind, although admittedly the last one I actually went to was Travis at the Birmingham NEC in 1999.

"Oh, why didn't I have Travis on instead of the Spice Girls? That's a shame."

Chinese swimmer's flippers and blowhole suspicious, says top official

...OME Olympians may be heavily-...isguised animals, it has been ...laimed.

The 16-year-old Chinese swim-...er Ye Shiwen, who smashed ...ecords in the 400 metres medley, ...as last seen heading out to sea at ...peeds of over 80 knots with her ...oach on her back.

Olympic official Roy Hobbs said: ...A younger swimmer can often ...nprove dramatically over a short ...eriod of time without recourse to

steroids but even the strongest attack of puberty doesn't usually cause somebody to start communicating via a series of clicks and squeaks.

"I'm not being cruel about her looks, she's far prettier than Frankie Boyle. But when a search of the changing rooms reveals a bucket of sprats and a zip-up rubber costume with a human face, I think it's reasonable to ask."

Recent advances in prosthetics have made it easier to disguise non-

human athletes. Earlier in the week Australian cyclist Tom Logan was revealed to be a wallaby.

Logan's team mate Stephen Malley said: "When Tom hit the ground his face, which had always had strange angles and a rubbery sheen, split open to revel a broad hairy muzzle. However I wasn't that surprised – absurdly large thigh muscles are par for the cycling course, but hopping and trying to mate with labradors less so."

GIRLS BITS!

STARS WITHOUT MAKEUP!

SIR ALEX REID
Alex recently raised over £20,000 for charity by tearing the head off a goat on live TV. We're not surprised he's looking a touch worse for wear! Well done son!

STEVE MCFADDEN
Eastender's Phil Mitchell was snapped clambering out from inside a large rhododendron in Southampton recently. Rumour has it he was trying to have a proper ruck with it.

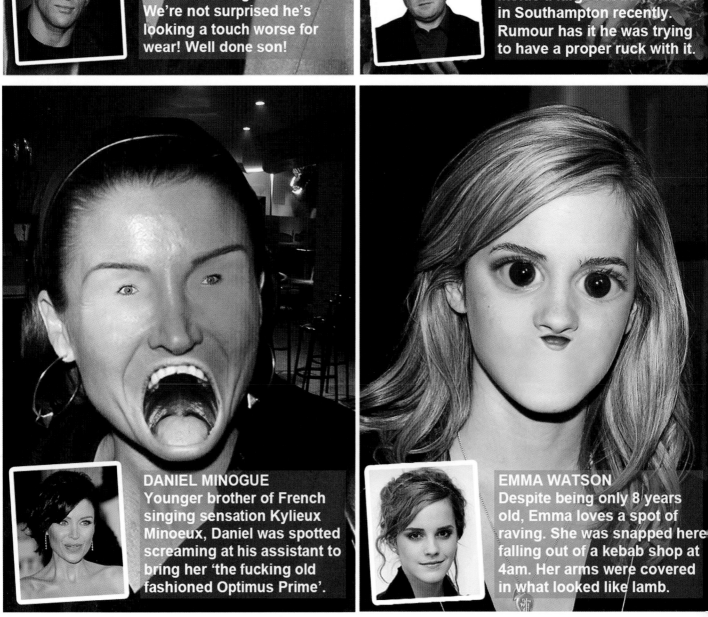

DANIEL MINOGUE
Younger brother of French singing sensation Kylieux Minoeux, Daniel was spotted screaming at his assistant to bring her 'the fucking old fashioned Optimus Prime'.

EMMA WATSON
Despite being only 8 years old, Emma loves a spot of raving. She was snapped here falling out of a kebab shop at 4am. Her arms were covered in what looked like lamb.